ATOMS

Building Blocks of Matter

These and other books are included in the
Encyclopedia of Discovery and Invention
series:

Airplanes: The Lure of Flight
Atoms: Building Blocks of Matter
Computers: Mechanical Minds
Gravity: The Universal Force
Lasers: Humanity's Magic Light
Printing Press: Ideas into Type
Radar: The Silent Detector
Television: Electronic Pictures

ATOMS

Building Blocks of Matter

by TIMOTHY LEVI BIEL

The ENCYCLOPEDIA of

D·I·S·C·O·V·E·R·Y
and INVENTION

Lucent Books, P.O. Box 289011 SAN DIEGO, CA 92198-0011

Library of Congress Cataloging-in-Publication Data

Biel, Timothy L.
    Atoms: building blocks of matter/by Timothy L. Biel.
      p. cm.— (The Encyclopedia of discovery and invention)
    Includes bibliographical references and index.
    Summary: Explores the history and development of atomic theory
from Democritus to Einstein and the present, presenting physics and
chemistry experiments done by famous scientists and discussing
nuclear power, fusion, and fission.
    ISBN 1-56006-207-X
    1. Matter—Constitution—Juvenile literature. 2. Atomic theory—
Juvenile literature. [1. Atomic theory. 2. Atoms structure.
3. Matter—Constitution.] I. Title. II. Series.
QC173.16.B54 1990
539.7—dc20   90-13214
                                                                  CIP
                                                                   AC

Contents

Foreword

The belief in progress has been one of the dominant forces in Western Civilization from the Scientific Revolution of the seventeenth century to the present. Embodied in the idea of progress is the conviction that each generation will be better off than the one that preceded it. Eventually, all peoples will benefit from and share in this better world. R. R. Palmer, in his *History of the Modern World*, calls this belief in progress "a kind of nonreligious faith that the conditions of human life" will continually improve as time goes on.

For over a thousand years prior to the seventeenth century, science had progressed little. Inquiry was largely discouraged, and experimentation almost nonexistent. As a result, science became regressive and discovery was ignored. Benjamin Farrington, a historian of science, characterized it this way: "Science had failed to become a real force in the life of society. Instead there had arisen a conception of science as a cycle of liberal studies for a privileged minority. Science ceased to be a means of transforming the conditions of life." In short, had this intellectual climate continued, humanity's future world would have been little more than a clone of its past.

Fortunately, these circumstances were not destined to last. By the seventeenth and eighteenth centuries, Western society was undergoing radical and favorable changes. And the changes that occurred gave rise to the notion that progress was a real force urging civilization forward. Surpluses of consumer goods were replacing substandard living conditions in most of Western Europe. Rigid class systems were giving way to social mobility. In nations like France and the United States, the lofty principles of democracy and popular sovereignty were being painted in broad, gilded strokes over the fading canvasses of monarchy and despotism.

But more significant than these social, economic, and political changes, the new age witnessed a rebirth of science. Centuries of scientific stagnation began crumbling before a spirit of scientific inquiry that spawned undreamed of technological advances. And it was the discoveries and inventions of scores of men and women that fueled these new technologies, dramatically increasing the ability of humankind to control nature—and, many believed, eventually to guide it.

It is a truism of science and technology that the results derived from observation and experimentation are not finalities. They are part of a process. Each discovery is but one piece in a continuum bridging past and present and heralding an extraordinary future. The heroic age of the Scientific Revolution was simply a start. It laid a foundation upon which succeeding generations of imaginative thinkers could build. It kindled the belief that progress is possible as long as there were gifted men and women who would respond to society's needs. When Antonie van Leeuwenhoek observed *Animalcules* (little animals) through his high-powered microscope in 1683, the discovery did not end there. Others followed who would call these "little animals" bacteria and, in time, recognize their role in the process of health and disease. Robert Koch, a German bacteriologist and winner of the Nobel prize in Physiology and Medicine, was one of these men. Koch firmly established that bacteria are responsible for causing infectious diseases. He identified, among others, the causative organisms of anthrax and tuberculosis. Alexander Fleming, another Nobel Laureate, progressed still further in the quest to understand and control bacteria. In 1928, Fleming discovered penicillin, the antibiotic wonder drug. Penicillin, and the generations of antibiotics that succeeded it, have done more to prevent premature death than any other discovery in the history of humankind. And as civilization hastens toward the twenty-first century, most agree that the conquest of van Leeuwenhoek's "little animals" will continue.

The *Encyclopedia of Discovery and Invention* examines those discoveries and inventions that have had a sweeping impact on life and thought in the modern world. Each book explores the ideas that led to the invention or discovery, and, more importantly, how the world changed and continues to change because of it. The series also highlights the people behind the achievements—the unique men and women whose singular genius and rich imagination have altered the lives of everyone. Enhanced by photographs and clearly explained technical drawings, these books are comprehensive examinations of the building blocks of human progress.

ATOMS

Building Blocks of Matter

ATOMS

Introduction

On the morning of August 6, 1945, an American B-29 bomber called the Enola Gay dropped the world's first atomic bomb. The deafening blast from the explosion and the fires that followed destroyed the city of Hiroshima, Japan. In an area measuring five square miles, only a handful of concrete buildings remained standing. The smell of burning flesh hung in the air.

Three days later, in the city of Nagasaki, about 190 miles south of Hiroshima, a second atomic bomb was dropped. Together, these two bombs took 210,000 lives and were the weapons used in the two most devastating bombings in military history. But that was not the end of the horror.

Months after the bombings, people in Hiroshima and Nagasaki became ill and died from the slow, painful effects of nuclear radiation produced by these bombs. Thousands more fled, hoping to escape the invisible evil that had invaded these two cities. For many, it was too late to escape. Cancer-causing radiation was already spreading through their bodies, and it usually led to death.

... TIMELINE: ATOMS

1 ■ 465 B.C.
Democritus born—the Greek philosopher who first suggested the world was made up of atoms.

2 ■ 384 B.C.
Aristotle theorizes that there are four basic elements of matter, earth, water, air and fire.

3 ■ 1609
Galileo presents evidence to dispute Aristotle's teachings, claiming that the earth and other planets revolve around the sun.

4 ■ 1661
Publication of *The Skeptical Chemist* by Robert Boyle.

5 ■ 1772
Antoine Lavoisier discovers the principle of combustion.

6 ■ 1803
John Dalton originates atomic theory, calculating some atomic weights and inventing chemical symbols.

7 ■ 1811
Avogadro proposes his theory of molecules.

8 ■ 1894
Sir William Crookes invents the electron tube or "Crookes tube."

9 ■ 1895
William Roentgen discovers X-rays.

10 ■ 1896
Radioactivity of uranium is discovered by Henri Becquerel.

In these horrible events, the world first witnessed the awesome power of the atom. The bombings of Hiroshima and Nagasaki marked the birth of the atomic age.

Today we live with the reality that nuclear weapons a hundred times more powerful than those dropped on Japan are aimed at virtually every major city in the world. We also realize that atomic power holds tremendous promise for peaceful use. It can provide the energy to run our factories and light our homes and cities. If controlled, radiation resulting from splitting the atom can help heal cancer rather than cause it.

Yet the atomic age is still in its infancy. We are just beginning to learn new technologies to help us tap the atom and to protect ourselves from its danger.

The atom is one of the oldest and most elusive mysteries in the history of science. There is no single moment in history when the atom was discovered or even a single year when its discovery took place. And no single person can be credited with discovering it. Instead, the atom's story is a slow unraveling that involves many scientists and their observations.

9 › 10 › 11 › 12 › 13 › 14 › 15 › 16 › 17 › 18 › 19 › 20 › 21 ›

11 ■ 1898
Discovery of radium by Pierre and Marie Curie.

12 ■ 1903
Radioactivity is explained by Ernest Rutherford.

13 ■ 1905
Albert Einstein introduces his theory of relativity.

14 ■ 1911
The "nuclear atom" is proposed by Rutherford.

15 ■ 1932
James Chadwick discovers the neutron.

16 ■ 1934
The first atomic nucleus splits, creating fission.

17 ■ 1939–45
World War II.

18 ■ 1945
First atomic bomb dropped on Hiroshima, Japan.

19 ■ 1963
Quark theory proposed.

20 ■ 1985
Atoms seen for the first time with a scanning tunneling microscope.

21 ■ 1986
Chernobyl nuclear reactor leaks radiation.

The Mysterious Atom

Knowledge of the atom, its structure and its power, is central to our modern way of life. Without this knowledge, there would be no television, radio, or other forms of electronic communication. No gasoline-powered vehicles or jet engines would have been invented. No plastic, cellophane, nylon, or other synthetic materials could have been manufactured. No records, no tapes, no movies would ever have been made. There would be no microwave ovens, lasers, or many of the other inventions we take for granted.

As important as the atom is to modern science and our modern way of life, its discovery was a torturously slow process. In fact, the story of its discovery is really a story of how modern science began. It begins over two thousand years ago in ancient Greece.

At that time, science was not the disciplined subject it is today. Early science was considered a form of magic and it was practiced by sorcerers and priests. They believed that nature was controlled by supernatural forces and that the only way to understand or manage nature was to appeal to these supernatural powers through magic. This tie between science, religion, and magic remained strong almost until the 1800s. But over the years, many philosophers and scientists have tried to break it. One of the first was a teacher named Democritus, who was born around 465 B.C. in Greece.

The First Atomic Theory

Democritus was the first person to suspect that atoms exist. In fact, it was Democritus who gave the atom its name, *Atomos.* In Greek it means "indivisible or unbreakable." Democritus's theory of the atom is simple, but even today it is basically correct.

Democritus noticed that when he rubbed a clod of dirt in his hands, it broke into smaller and smaller pieces. When he picked up one of these small

The ancient Greek philosopher Democritus, who lived in the fifth century B.C., believed matter was made up of indivisible units, or "atoms" in Greek. Though Democritus's atomic theory was very simple, it was basically correct.

pieces and rubbed it between his fingers, it, too, broke into smaller and smaller particles. Democritus reasoned that if he could have picked up one of these tiny particles, it, too, could be broken into smaller and smaller pieces.

But eventually, Democritus speculated, the clod would be broken into its smallest possible pieces and could not be broken any more. He called these pieces atoms and believed that all the matter in the world is made from them.

Democritus thought that there were hundreds of different kinds of atoms and that each one joined with others of its own kind to make up all the different forms of matter. He speculated that some matter was made of hard, rough atoms packed so closely together that they were almost impossible to take apart. These atoms, claimed Democritus, made up rocks and metals. Other atoms must be smooth and slippery, he believed. When thousands of slippery atoms were heaped together, they slipped and slid over one another. This mass of atoms would flow in the form of a liquid. Still other atoms, he thought, must be slippery like water, but much lighter. They would not only flow in all directions but would float above the earth as well. He believed these atoms formed the air we breathe.

According to Democritus, atoms were eternal and indestructible. He maintained that they had always existed and would continue to exist forever. Although a single atom could combine with other atoms or be broken away from them, the atom itself could never be changed or destroyed. This, he believed, was a permanent law of nature.

Aristotle and the Disappearance of the Atom

So, two thousand years ago, Democritus had understood several basic concepts of the atom. Unfortunately, another influential early scientist completely disagreed with Democritus. This was Aristotle, one of the most important philosophers of all time. Aristotle was born in 384 B.C., about one hundred years after Democritus. His teachings and writings became so influential over the next two thousand years that most people simply referred to him as "the philosopher."

Aristotle was an early spokesman for the scientific method. He taught people to distrust the prophecies and divine revelations so popular in his

The Greek philosopher Aristotle proposed a theory of matter based on what the senses alone could perceive. Since the five senses could not perceive atoms, Aristotle rejected Democritus's theory.

time. Instead, he believed people should trust their senses. Aristotle urged his students to examine the world around them with their own eyes and to feel, weigh, taste, and smell it. Through their physical senses, he believed, they would arrive at truth.

Around 350 B.C. he recorded his own examination of the physical world and established his interpretation of the laws of nature in a work entitled *The Physics*. At the time, it was the most thorough scientific study of nature that anyone had ever attempted. And for almost two thousand years, *The Physics* of Aristotle remained the unquestioned authority in the Western world on all scientific matters.

It was because Aristotle placed complete trust in the human senses that he disagreed with Democritus. He refused to believe that any form of matter existed that could not be seen, felt, or otherwise sensed. He proposed his own theory about the composition of matter.

Aristotle's Four Elements

Aristotle examined hundreds of different materials and classified them according to their physical characteristics—solid, liquid, or gas, hardness, weight, and density. Based on his observations, he claimed that all differences in matter resulted from a combination of just two conditions: heat and moisture. From these two conditions, he derived what he called the four basic elements of nature: earth, water, air, and fire. An element is a substance that cannot be broken down into any other substance.

Each element in Aristotle's system was a pure combination of the two conditions. Earth was the cold, dry element, water was cold and wet. Air was hot and moist, while fire was hot and dry. Based on his logic, Aristotle believed that every different kind of matter was just a different combination of these four elements.

The beauty of Aristotle's system is that it is based entirely on the senses. While Democritus had proposed that matter could be broken down into invisible atoms, Aristotle believed that matter cannot be broken down any further than the four visible elements.

Aristotle even introduced the idea of elementary chemistry. It taught that matter can be changed by altering the proportions of the four elements that are found in every substance. Changing one substance into another was simple: you just add or remove heat and moisture. The perfect examples of this were steam, water, and ice. These, according to Aristotle, were three different substances. When water is heated, it takes on more fire and air and becomes steam. When it is frozen, it gives up these elements for more earth and becomes ice.

Although Aristotle's physics were primitive and inaccurate, they provided the first system that people used to analyze, compare, and classify matter. For nearly two thousand years, people in the Western world accepted Aristotle's four elements as the basic building blocks of nature.

The Church Enshrines Aristotle's Physics

After the decline of the Greek and Roman empires, science and learning came to a standstill in western Europe.

A fifteenth-century woodcut depicts the belief that the senses were untrustworthy since the devil could deceive them. Therefore, a person was on safer ground trusting in divine revelation as taught by the Bible and the church.

Between the fifth and eighth centuries A.D., most of the wisdom of the Greeks and Romans was lost during a period called the Dark Ages. For centuries, churches were the only centers of learning, and they taught that truth came from God through the Bible and through its interpretations by priests. For nearly a thousand years, the church controlled all the universities and most of the learning in Europe. Whenever someone offered physical evidence that disagreed with the church's official teachings, church scholars dismissed it. They argued that divine revelation through God was more reliable than the physical senses. In fact, they taught that the

devil often used our senses to tempt us or trick us.

For the little science they did teach, church scholars used their own peculiar interpretations of Aristotle's physics. They ignored his insistence on observing the physical world with the senses. However, his theory of the four elements fit almost perfectly into their view of the world, but they added a fifth element called quintessence to the theory. Quintessence was the perfect blend of the other four elements. It was from this divine substance that God created the earth and its four elements.

Medieval Alchemists Try to Improve upon Nature

During the Middle Ages, approximately A.D. 800 to 1350, the church retained its control over learning, and Aristotle's physics remained the basis of natural science. However, some people experimented with ways to separate and recombine Aristotle's four elements. This early form of chemistry was called alchemy and was practiced by people called alchemists.

Early alchemists performed experiments by consulting astrological charts. Performing an experiment under the right sign was as important as or more important than using the right ingredients.

These alchemists built elaborate furnaces and baths in which to heat and soak materials. They believed that in this way they could alter the proportions of earth, fire, air, and water and change one substance into another. The alchemists' goal was to purify matter. To them this meant changing a base, or impure, substance like lead

Medieval alchemists use a bath and a furnace to change one substance into another.

or iron into a purer substance, such as silver, mercury, or gold. They called this kind of alteration transmutation. They believed the ultimate transmutation would be to create the perfect element of quintessence.

In spite of their superstitions and mistaken ambitions, some of these alchemists were careful scientists. They recorded the portions of materials they used in their experiments. They described the weight, texture, hardness, density, and color of the materials they used and how these were changed when burned, mixed, or soaked in different liquids.

As the goal of creating silver, mercury, or gold became more and more obviously impossible, the alchemists' experiments cast doubt on Aristotle's four elements.

For example, Roger Bacon, a thirteenth-century alchemist, was the first person to recognize that fire cannot exist without air. He wondered how fire could be considered an element if it cannot exist independently. By the fifteenth century, many alchemists were criticizing Aristotle's theories. The Swiss alchemist Paracelsus, perhaps the most famous of all alchemists, urged his col-

Alchemists work busily to create healing potions and brews to treat inmates of a medieval children's hospital.

Paracelsus was perhaps the most famous alchemist of his era. Many of his theories were scientifically sound and some of his medicinal compounds are still in use today. Other physicians of his time often considered his theories radical and dangerous.

leagues to separate, or refine, materials to determine their usefulness in healing.

Slowly the emphasis of alchemy changed from combining elements to make gold to separating substances into their fundamental parts. Paracelsus identified sulfur, mercury, iron, and arsenic as substances that could not be broken down any further. No matter what chemical action they underwent and no matter how small their quantities, they retained the same qualities. Paracelsus had identified four elements, although he did not call them that.

A German contemporary of Paracelsus, who went by the name of Agricola, introduced methods for separating metals from the ore, or rock, in which they appear naturally. In great detail he described his method for mining, separating, and refining such metals as iron, tin, lead, silver, and gold. Although they still called themselves al-

chemists, Paracelsus and Agricola were lifting the veil of superstition from chemistry and replacing it with the mantle of science. In the next century, an Italian alchemist, Giambattista Della Porta, advanced the cause of science even further by making the world's first magnifying glass.

The Telescope and Microscope Reveal "Invisible" Worlds

The art of grinding glass to make lenses that magnified objects proved to be a great turning point in science. For example, by grinding glass Galileo, the great Italian astronomer, was able to

Italian astronomer Galileo Galilei peers through his invention, the telescope. With the telescope, Galileo was able to determine that the earth moved around the sun. His discovery almost cost him his life at the hands of church authorities.

In the sixteenth century, the newly developed art of grinding glass enabled scientists like Galileo to make magnifying lenses. With such lenses, Galileo constructed the telescope pictured here. What he saw with it changed the world.

build the first functional telescope. With it, Galileo helped to topple another of Aristotle's views—the belief that the sun, stars, and other planets revolve around the earth. Church leaders found his teachings so threatening that they had Galileo arrested, tortured, and threatened with death. Finally, in a public trial in 1632, Galileo was forced to renounce his findings, convinced that it was the only way his life would be spared.

It was too late, however, for the church to halt the avalanche of inquiry and questioning that Galileo had started. His book *Star Messenger* had become well known, and its message was clear: vast new worlds awaited exploration, worlds that had previously been invisible to the naked eye.

Not all the new worlds to be explored were out in space. One of Galileo's contemporaries was Pierre Gassendi, a French philosopher and scientist. Gassendi, too, was a vocal critic of Aristotle, but fearing the same fate that had

befallen Galileo, he kept his criticisms to himself. When he died in 1658, Gassendi's writings were made public. They contained a theory of the atom remarkably similar to the forgotten theory of Democritus. Gassendi, however, added a new touch that turned out to be amazingly prophetic. He speculated that invisible forces act between atoms much like magnetic forces act between metals. These forces, thought Gassendi, are what cause some atoms to attract each other and stick together and other atoms to repel one another.

One of the first people to recognize the importance of Gassendi's work was the great English physicist Sir Isaac Newton, the discoverer of gravity. Like Gassendi, Newton believed that all things,

Sixteenth-century French philosopher and scientist Pierre Gassendi disagreed with Aristotle's views concerning matter. Gassendi formulated an atomic theory resembling that of Democritus and speculated that there were magnetic attractions between atoms.

Seventeenth-century English physicist Sir Isaac Newton performs an experiment with light. Newton's study of matter and the forces of nature led him to believe that all things, including light, were composed of atoms.

Just as magnifying lenses allowed astronomers to view extraterrestrial bodies, such lenses also enabled scientists to see things too small for the naked eye to see. The early microscope pictured here was built to study the circulation of blood.

even light, were composed of atoms. In 1681 he wrote:

> It seems probable to me, that God in the Beginning form'd Matter in solid, massy, hard, impenetrable, moveable Particles, of such Sizes and Figures, and with such other Properties, and in such Proportion, as most conduced to the End for which He form'd them; and that these primitive Particles being Solids, are incomparably harder than any porous Bodies compounded of them; even so very hard as never to wear or break in Pieces, no ordinary Power being able to divide what God Himself made one in the first Creation.

Miniature Worlds

It was the invention of the microscope that next revealed particles in matter that had been invisible before. In 1676,

a Dutchman named Antonie van Leeuwenhoek wrote a letter to the Royal Society of London, a newly-formed society of scientists. In his letter, van Leeuwenhoek stated that he had used a microscope to observe water, and in a drop of water, he had discovered tiny living things. He called these creatures, which were invisible to the naked eye, *animalcules*. The most important thing about Leeuwenhoek's work is that he proved that particles of matter too small to see with the naked eye do exist. His work triggered a new interest in the microscope and the miniature world it

Dutch scientist Antonie van Leeuwenhoek invented the microscope in the seventeenth century. With it he discovered microscopic organisms living in a drop of water. He thus proved that things too small for the unaided senses to detect do exist.

revealed. Soon scientists around the world were using microscopes to reveal intricate patterns never seen before— the patterns of a butterfly's wing, a sea shell, or of crystals in copper and other metals.

A Skeptical Chemist

Aristotle's theories, then, were being slowly toppled by people like Gassendi and van Leeuwenhoek. But the man who is credited with finally disproving Aristotle is Robert Boyle, a wealthy English nobleman with a passion for science. In 1661, Boyle published a book entitled *The Skeptical Chemist,* in which he disproved the theory of the four elements and the quintessence. He also explained why creating gold from another metal is impossible.

Boyle claimed that gold is an element, so it can be neither made nor unmade. Elements can be created only by nature, he asserted. In *The Skeptical Chemist,* he described hundreds of experiments that he had performed to combine or separate natural substances. From these he determined that iron, tin, lead, silver, copper, mercury, sulfur, and arsenic are also elements. Other substances, like salt, water, and glass, Boyle defined as compounds, or substances formed from two or more elements. Boyle believed that the exact proportions of elements in a particular compound always remain constant. He further believed that a process of chemical analysis could be developed to determine what these proportions are.

Seventeenth century English scientist Robert Boyle's chemical experiments proved that many individual elements existed in nature—not just the four named by Aristotle. Boyle also recognized that these elements combined to form compounds.

ELEMENTS AND COMPOUNDS

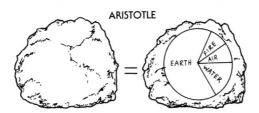

ARISTOTLE

EARTH / FIRE / AIR / WATER

Late in the nineteenth century Antoine Lavoisier replaced the old Aristotelean idea of elements with the modern concept of elements and compounds. According to Aristotle, all substances on earth contained a mixture of four elements, earth, fire, air, and water, as shown above. In place of these four elements, Lavoisier identified about twenty substances he called elements. He defined an element as a substance that will not break down into different substances.

Elements combine in exact proportions with other elements to form all the compounds on earth. The proportions of elements in two common compounds are shown below. You can see how a compound differs from an element, such as gold. No matter how much you try to break an element down, it does not change.

LAVOISIER

WATER	=	1 PART HYDROGEN / 8 PARTS OXYGEN
SALT	=	46 PARTS SODIUM / 71 PARTS CHLORINE
GOLD	=	GOLD

Lavoisier, the Father of Modern Chemistry

Like many original thinkers, Boyle had little success in convincing his fellow scientists that his theory was correct. More than a century after his death, most people still believed that there were only four elements in nature. It took the exhaustive efforts of the bril-liant French chemist Antoine Lavoisier to prove that Boyle was right.

Lavoisier was a brilliant, energetic, and meticulous chemist. In his work he set out to build the system of chemical elements that Boyle had formulated. He carefully weighed and labeled the ingredients and resulting substances of each of his experiments. Lavoisier was able to write the names, weights, and

Antoine Lavoisier, the father of modern chemistry, established a sound scientific method for conducting experiments. He discovered the principle of combustion; that is, that when something burns, it combines with oxygen.

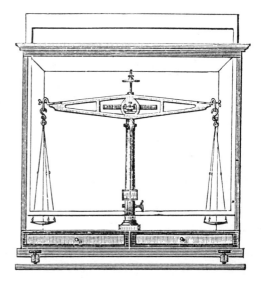

A scale, or balance, became Lavoisier's most important tool in the laboratory. With it he weighed the ingredients and end-products of his experiments, enabling him to determine the chemical change that had taken place.

measurements of elements and compounds. Lavoisier made the chemist's scale the most important instrument in his lab, and in doing so he laid the groundwork for modern chemistry.

In one of his most famous experiments, Lavoisier discovered the princi-

A seventeenth century painting of Antoine Lavoisier and the two loves of his life, his wife and his work.

ple of combustion, or, what happens to an object when it burns. First he weighed a piece of sulfur and then placed it in a beaker. Next he set the sulfur on fire and sealed the beaker so that it would capture the smoke and gases the sulfur gave off. After the sulfur had burned, he weighed the smoke, gases, and waste products.

From this simple experiment, Lavoisier drew several important conclusions. First he established that the smoke, gases, and waste products actually weighed more than the original piece of sulfur. Lavoisier repeated his experiment several times, and each time the weight after burning the sulfur increased by exactly the same amount. Lavoisier concluded that when something burns, it combines with oxygen and becomes a gas. Since the sulfur, for example, had combined with oxygen, it had to weigh more than the original sulfur alone.

A drawing of Antoine Lavoisier and his equipment for separating water into its components.

On November 1, 1772, Lavoisier wrote a letter to the French Academy of Sciences describing his experiments. In it he included a mathematical equation showing exactly what weights of sulfur and oxygen had been combined and what weights of gases and other waste by-products were produced. He had written the world's first chemical equation.

Lavoisier's equation described a chemical reaction. He defined a chemical reaction as a process in which elements are rearranged to form new compounds or are freed from compounds, and he introduced the equation as the way to describe these reactions. He also stated an important law that governs all chemical reactions: the law of conservation of matter. According to this law, matter can change forms, but it can never be created or destroyed. That is why the total weight on both sides of a chemical equation must be exactly the same.

Lavoisier was the most important scientist of his day. His work confirmed Boyle's definitions of elements and compounds. His objective was to identify all the natural elements in the world. Before his untimely death in 1794, he had succeeded in naming about twenty elements and writing equations for the most common compounds that these elements formed. Included in Lavoisier's list of elements were hydrogen, oxygen, nitrogen, carbon, sulfur, phosphorus, gold, silver, tin, and several other metals.

Lavoisier's Tragic Death

One can only wonder how many more important discoveries this brilliant scientist might have made if his life had not come to a sudden end in 1794. It was the fifth year after the French Revolution, during what is known as the Reign of Terror, in France. The revolutionary leaders had overthrown the French nobility, executed King Louis XVI, and were rounding up all former tax collectors who had helped the nobility in oppressing the poor.

A painting of the execution by guillotine of King Louis XVI of France in 1793. The brilliant career of Antoine Lavoisier came to the same grisly end in 1794. French revolutionists executed him for his partnership in a tax-collecting firm. They put little value on his great contributions to science.

Unfortunately, Lavoisier had been a partner in a tax collecting firm, from which he had profited quite handsomely. He was among those arrested on May 7, 1794, and the next day he was interrogated. He and the other tax collectors were allowed fifteen minutes to prepare their defense. Lavoisier argued that he had rendered his country a great service as a scientist, but the judge interrupted him: "The Republic doesn't need scientists!" Lavoisier was executed on the guillotine a few hours later.

By the time of Lavoisier's death, the science of chemistry had emerged completely from the shadow of Aristotle. The fundamental concepts of elements and compounds had been established and proved. Chemists who followed Lavoisier in the early 1800s experimen-ted with one chemical reaction after another. They discovered the exact proportions of elements in common compounds such as salt, sugar, acids, wood, cotton, and blood.

This contributed not only to science but also to industry. For the first time, chemists could combine elements in exact proportions and produce predicted compounds. The manufacture of dyes and soaps were two of the earliest commercial successes resulting from this chemical process.

This was just the beginning of a scientific and industrial revolution that would sweep the world in the next century. But before that revolution could proceed, scientists still had to answer a fundamental question: What are elements made of?

A Mystery Solved

Before he died in 1794, Lavoisier had shown that a chemical compound can be formed only by a chemical reaction such as combustion. He had also demonstrated that to create a specific compound by chemical reaction, the elements must be combined in the right proportions. For instance, the weight of the oxygen that goes into water is exactly 8 times more than that of hydrogen. It is never 7.9 or 8.1 times heavier. It is always exactly 8 times more.

Dalton's Atomic Theory

The English physicist and chemist John Dalton was fascinated by these proportions. Born in 1766 as the son of a poor Quaker farmer, Dalton's gift for learning was soon recognized throughout his small village. At the age of twelve, he started to teach in his village school. By nineteen he had become the principal of the school, and his reputation as a brilliant scholar spread. But because of his family's religion, he was barred from teaching at England's most prestigious universities.

Finally, Dalton received an appointment to teach at a small, private college. There, working with a microscope for the first time, he became intrigued by crystals. Others had already observed that all the crystals of a particular element or compound have a unique geometric form. Crystals of copper, for

English physicist and chemist John Dalton's religious beliefs barred him from teaching in a major university. But he nonetheless went on to formulate the leading atomic theory of his day.

example, are always in the shape of squares; quartz crystals are shaped like six-sided prisms; and the crystals of garnet look like miniature pyramids.

What Dalton was most curious about, however, was how crystals are formed and why they form in unique geometric patterns. No one had been able to explain that until Dalton spent several years studying these mysterious shapes. Then, in 1808, he reached an astounding conclusion. It turned out to be one of the most important breakthroughs in the history of science.

Dalton concluded that there could be only one reason for crystals to form the way they do: atoms. He argued that crystals form in specific patterns because they are arrangements of atoms, and some unidentified force or power of attraction in the atoms themselves causes them to be arranged in these patterns.

Although he could not identify the force that attracts atoms to one another, Dalton did suggest a way to prove that atoms exist. His suggestion was to weigh them. Obviously, a single atom is too small to weigh, but Dalton believed that the proportions of elements in a compound could reflect the weight of their atoms.

John Dalton's table of elements of 1803 used symbols to represent the elements as well as assigning each element an atomic weight relative to the weight of hydrogen to which he gave a weight of one.

ELEMENTS

		Wt				Wt
⊙	Hydrogen.	1	⊕	Strontian		46
⊕	Azote	5	✳	Barytes		68
●	Carbon	54	Ⓘ	Iron		50
○	Oxygen	7	Ⓩ	Zinc		56
⊗	Phosphorus	9	Ⓒ	Copper		56
⊕	Sulphur	13	Ⓛ	Lead		90
⊘	Magnesia	20	Ⓢ	Silver		190
⊖	Lime	24	Ⓖ	Gold		190
◫	Soda	28	Ⓟ	Platina		190
⦿	Potash	42	✷	Mercury		167

Take water, for example. It was known that for every eight parts of oxygen in water there is exactly one part of hydrogen. According to Dalton, the smallest particle of water would contain one atom of oxygen and one atom of hydrogen. He called this a compounded atom of water. If a compounded atom of water contains a single atom of hydrogen and a single atom of oxygen, then an atom of oxygen must weigh eight times more than one atom of hydrogen.

Dalton's logic was brilliant. He had observed, as had many other chemists, that only one element can combine with another element in the same proportion. Only oxygen, for example, can combine with hydrogen in a ratio of 8 ounces to 1 ounce. Another element may combine with hydrogen in a ratio of 2 to 1, still another at 3 to 1, and yet another at 4 to 1. But only oxygen will combine at the ratio of 8 to 1. And it will combine only with hydrogen at that ratio.

Therefore, Dalton concluded, the atom of every single element must have its own unique weight. By knowing the proportions in which two or more elements combine to form a compound, one can figure out their relative weights. Dalton called this an element's atomic weight. Since hydrogen appeared to be the lightest element, he assigned hydrogen the atomic weight of 1, oxygen the atomic weight of 8, and so on. It is its unique atomic weight, claimed Dalton, that gives each element its unique properties. Every atom of hydrogen, for example, is identical to every other hydrogen atom, but these atoms differ from the atoms of sulfur, which differ from the atoms of gold, and so on.

For the rest of his life, Dalton searched for the secret force that binds

AN ATOMIC WEIGHT CHECKLIST

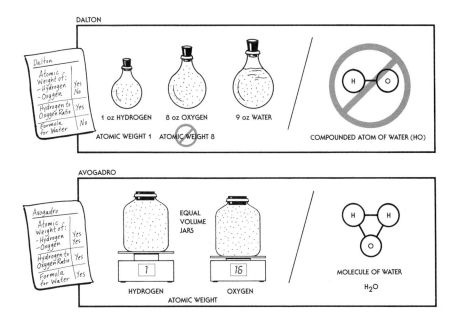

DALTON

Dalton		
Atomic Weight of:		
–Hydrogen	Yes	
–Oxygen	No	
Hydrogen to Oxygen Ratio	Yes	
Formula for Water	No	

1 oz HYDROGEN — ATOMIC WEIGHT 1

8 oz OXYGEN — ATOMIC WEIGHT 8

9 oz WATER

COMPOUNDED ATOM OF WATER (HO)

AVOGADRO

Avogadro		
Atomic Weight of:		
–Hydrogen	Yes	
–Oxygen	Yes	
Hydrogen to Oxygen Ratio	Yes	
Formula for Water	Yes	

EQUAL VOLUME JARS

HYDROGEN 1 · OXYGEN 16 · ATOMIC WEIGHT

MOLECULE OF WATER H_2O

John Dalton's theory of atomic weight offered the first evidence that the atom exists. His recognition that the proportions of elements in a compound reflect the weight of their atoms was an important breakthrough. Dalton established the atomic weight of hydrogen, the lightest element, as 1. However, he assumed that a "compound atom" could only contain one atom of each element in the compound. For example, he mistakenly believed the formula for water was HO, one atom of hydrogen and one of oxygen. Since the oxygen in water outweighs the hydrogen 8 to 1, Dalton believed that oxygen had an atomic weight of 8.

A few years later, Avogadro established his important law. According to this law, a gallon jar filled with hydrogen contains exactly as many atoms as a gallon jar filled with oxygen. Avogadro found that a gallon of oxygen weighs 16 times more than a gallon of hyrdogen, so he concluded that an atom of oxygen must weigh 16 times more than an atom of hydrogen. That means the atomic weight of oxygen is 16, not 8 as Dalton had believed.

But Dalton had shown correctly that oxygen always combines with hydrogen in the ratio of parts of oxygen to 1 part of hydrogen. The only way this was possible, Avogadro concluded, was for a molecule of water to contain two atoms of hydrogen and one atom of oxygen. Thus, Avogadro was able to give both the correct atomic weight for oxygen and the correct formula for water—H_2O.

atoms together. Like Lavoisier, he looked for clues by examining the weights of elements, but he had made one assumption that led him slightly off track. Dalton assumed that a compounded atom could contain only a single atom from each element present in the compound. He wrote the formula for water, for example, as H+O=HO. In other words, according to Dalton, an atom of hydrogen plus an atom of oxygen yields one compounded atom of water. Since he knew that it takes eight ounces of oxygen and one ounce of hydrogen to make nine ounces of water, Dalton concluded that every oxygen atom must weigh exactly eight times more than a single hydrogen atom.

His only mistake was assuming that each element in a compound can contribute only one atom per compounded atom. He did not allow for the possibility that a compound might contain more atoms of one element than another. For example, if water contains two atoms of hydrogen for every atom of oxygen, then the atomic weight of oxygen has to be 16, not 8.

How Do You Weigh an Atom?

In other respects, his concept of a compounded atom was correct. Each compounded atom, or the smallest particle of a compound, had to be identical, each one containing exactly the same number of atoms of each element. In fact, his idea of atomic weight became the basis for comparing different elements.

Intrigued by Dalton's ideas, an Italian physicist named Amedeo Avogadro found a way to compare atomic weights more accurately in 1811. He started by studying the properties of gases, such as hydrogen, helium, nitrogen, and oxygen. After recording the weight and volume of thousands of gas samples, he discovered something remarkable about all gases. As he stated it: "If gases of any kind are put into vessels of equal size, as long as their temperature and pressure remain the same, the vessels will contain the same number of gas particles." Other scientists tested this theory and found it to be true. Soon it became known as Avogadro's law.

To put this important law in simpler terms, if you filled a one gallon jar with hydrogen and an identical jar with oxygen, and made sure you kept both jars at the same temperature and air pressure, the jar of hydrogen would contain exactly the same number of atoms as the jar of oxygen.

With this discovery, Avogadro could take Dalton's idea of atomic weight one step further. He could now figure out the exact atomic weights of many gases. When Avogadro compared equal jars of hydrogen and oxygen, for example, he discovered that the oxygen jar weighed sixteen times more than the hydrogen jar. Therefore, he concluded, an atom of oxygen must weigh sixteen times more than an atom of hydrogen. If the atomic weight of hydrogen is 1, then oxygen has an atomic weight of 16.

Next Avogadro applied his findings to Dalton's idea of compounded atoms. If the amount of oxygen in water is only eight times more than the amount of hydrogen, why does water weigh sixteen times as much? The only possible answer is that each compounded atom of water contains two atoms of hydrogen and one atom of oxygen. Avogadro wrote the formula for this compounded atom as H_2O.

Italian physicist Amedeo Avogadro (1776-1856) further developed Dalton's theory of atomic weights. Avogadro figured out that if different gases were kept in the same size jars at the same pressure and temperature they would contain the same number of atoms.

Avogadro also gave these compounded atoms a new name. He called them molecules, which is Italian for "little masses."

Avogadro's method of comparing atomic weights was the missing clue that enabled chemists to assign exact atomic weights to all the known elements. It was like putting together the pieces of an enormous jigsaw puzzle. The more chemists tested and analyzed compounds, the more pieces of the puzzle fit into place. Hydrogen, the lightest element in the world, was given an atomic weight of 1. The next lightest element is helium, which weighs four times more than hydrogen, so its atomic weight is 4. Oxygen's atomic weight is 16, iron's is 56. The heaviest element that occurs in nature is uranium, with an atomic weight of 238.

Mendeleev's Periodic Table Silences the Doubters

Nearly fifty years after Avogadro's work with atomic weights, the theory of the atom was still not universally accepted. Even highly respected chemists doubted its existence. They could not disprove Avogadro's or Dalton's idea of proportional weights, but they argued that these proportions may not be caused by atoms. As late as 1855, Jean Baptiste Dumas, one of the most respected chemists in the world, declared: "I absolutely refuse to believe what I cannot see or picture in my mind."

In 1869, the meticulous and brilliant work of a Russian chemist, Dmitri Mendeleev, provided undeniable proof that the distinct atomic weights of the elements is what accounts for the differences in their physical and chemical properties. He started by listing all sixty-three known elements in order of their atomic weight, from the lightest to the heaviest.

When he began to analyze and compare the physical and chemical properties of the elements thus listed, he noticed a surprising phenomenon. Every eight elements on his list, arranged strictly by atomic weight, had remarkably similar characteristics. For example, lithium, the third element on his list, is a silvery white, soft metal. So is the eleventh element, potassium, the nineteenth, rubidium, and the twenty-seventh, cesium. Not only do they look and feel similar but they also have almost identical melting and boiling points, and they combine chemically with the same elements. Only the weight proportions in these compounds are different.

I	MINERÆ							
II	METALLA							
III	MINERALIA		Bismuth	Zinck	Marcasit	Kobolt	Zaffra	Magnesia	Magnes
IV	SALIA							Borax	Chrysocolla
V	DECOMPOSITA							
VI	TERRÆ		Crocus	Crocus	Vitrum	Vitrum	Minium Lithargirum	Cadmia Tutia	Ochra Schmelta
VII	DESTILLATA							
VIII	OLEA		Ol			Butyr	Liquor Silicum	Ol Thenben
IX	LIMI	C.V. ψ	Arena Glares	Creta Rubrica	Terra Sigillata Bolus	Hæmatites Smiris	Talcum	Granati	Asbestus
X	COMPOSITIONES	Fluxus Niger	Fluxus Albus		Coloriza	Decoctio	Tirapelle	

An early table of elements for use in the laboratory reflects chemistry's roots in alchemy. Many of the symbols used in the table have their origin in astrology.

Mendeleev found such a remarkable consistency in this periodic repetition of properties that he stated it in the form of a law, which we now call the periodic law: "The elements arranged according to their atomic weight show a periodic change of properties." Based on this law, he created the very first periodic table of the elements in 1869.

The periodic table is arranged according to this repetition of properties. The first column, for example, contains the so-called alkali metals—lithium (Li), sodium (Na), potassium (K), rubidium (Rb), and cesium (Cs). All are silvery white, soft metals, which tarnish rapidly when exposed to air, and which are good conductors of electricity. The last column in the periodic table contains the so-called noble gases—helium (He), neon (Ne), argon (Ar), krypton (Kr), xenon (Xe), and radon (Rn). They are called noble because they rarely mingle with other elements to form compounds. A short column in the middle of the table contains the so-called coinage metals—copper (Cu), silver (Ag), and gold (Au).

Mendeleev found such an astonishing consistency that when he found an

Russian chemistry professor Dmitri Mendeleev discovered that every eighth element in a table of elements had similar properties. He arranged his table according to this periodicity of elements. By doing so, he was able to predict the existence of yet undiscovered elements.

Mendeleev ponders the wonders of the material world in which he discerned a strict logic that governs the elements. His periodic law was the final proof that convinced science to replace Aristotle's theory of four elements with an atomic theory.

inconsistency, he assumed that a missing element had not yet been discovered. Basing his predictions on his periodic law, he anticipated the discovery of several elements, and he predicted their atomic weight, density, melting and boiling points, and how they would react with oxygen, chlorine, and other elements. In almost every case, the missing element has been discovered, and it fits Mendeleev's predicted characteristics.

The periodic table was the final proof of Dalton's atomic theory. It allowed scientists to replace Aristotle's four elements—earth, air, water, and fire—with an accurate list of over sixty elements. Yet no one knew why the periodic table worked. Chemists were able to predict the outcome of chemical reactions with incredible accuracy, even though all they really knew about the atoms involved was their weight relative to an atom of hydrogen. The image of the atom that evolved was of a solid little sphere. It would be another forty years before that image changed. In the meantime chemists wondered about another mystery: How is it that some substances occur as gases, others as liquids, and still others as solids?

What Is Heat?

The first clue came in 1827, when an English botanist, Robert Brown, examined a drop of water under a microscope. Brown noticed that tiny specks in the water were constantly trembling and vibrating. At first Brown believed he had discovered a new form of one-celled plant or animal life, tinier than any living organism previously discovered. He carefully saved the water in a

English botanist Robert Brown (1773-1858) lent his name to the phenomenon of molecular movement called Brownian motion. Brown was the first to notice that molecules were in constant motion. Scientists later realized that molecular motion was the cause of heat production.

culture, hoping that he could make a whole colony of these microscopic creatures grow.

Try as he might, Brown could not make anything grow from the samples he had taken. Nevertheless, he reported his findings to other scientists. Many of them noticed the same movement in water that Brown had detected, and it came to be known as Brownian motion. But no one could explain the movement, and Brownian motion remained a mystery for more than seventy years.

It was not solved until the end of the century, when scientists realized that Brownian motion had nothing to do with living organisms. Instead, they discovered that Brownian motion is the movement of the water molecules themselves. Another name for this movement is heat. For as scientists had discovered, heat is simply the movement of molecules. All atoms and molecules, whether in gases, liquids, or solids, have some heat, or motion. The faster an object's molecules are moving, the warmer that object is. When you touch something that feels hot, like a burner on your stove, what you are actually feeling is the pounding of the burner's fast-moving molecules against your skin.

Gases, Liquids, and Solids

Two conflicting forces cause different materials to appear as gases, liquids, or solids. One of these forces is heat. The hotter an object is, the faster its molecules are moving. The random movement of molecules drives them apart. But heat is countered by a mysterious force of attraction that holds molecules together.

Some molecules bind together more strongly than others. These are the molecules of substances that appear in nature as solids. It takes a great amount of heat to melt these materials, or turn them into liquids, and even more heat is required to get them to boil, or turn to gas. Most kinds of materials in nature are solids. Their molecules have such a strong attraction to one another that they form rigid, geometric shapes, called crystals.

The molecules in gases, on the other hand, have weak bonds. They float about freely with just enough attraction to one another to form shapeless masses or to fill up a closed container. Some of the molecules in a gas are constantly escaping and floating away. Only the earth's gravity prevents these gases from floating infinitely into space. Gravity holds gases, most notably nitrogen, oxygen, carbon dioxide, and helium, within about eighty miles of the earth's surface, forming the mixture of gases we call air.

Only one element appears naturally as a liquid, and that is mercury. However, many compounds occur as liquids, including the earth's most abundant substance, water. As you can guess, the molecules of water and other liquids have stronger molecular bonds than gases have but a weaker attraction than solids have. Liquids do not have a rigid structure like solids have, but unlike gases their molecules do adhere well enough to hold them together. These are the characteristics that make it possible to pour a liquid or make it fit the shape of its container.

Most substances can be converted from one state of matter to another by heating them. By making its molecules move faster, a substance can be changed from a solid to a liquid, or from a liquid to a gas. Heat water over 212 de-

The S.S. Clermont *steams its way up the Hudson River in New York in the early nineteenth century. American artist and inventor Robert Fulton (1765-1815) engineered the* Clermont, *the first commercially successful steam-powered ship in America.*

grees Fahrenheit, for instance, and it turns to steam. Cool it, or slow its molecules down to 32 degrees Fahrenheit, and it will turn to ice.

The Invisible Dynamo

By the middle of the nineteenth century, steam engines in factories powered machines that produced more goods than ever before. Steamships and locomotives transported these goods around the world faster than ever before. The Industrial Revolution was in high gear. While most of the credit for this revolution is usually given to the invention of the steam engine, the new knowledge of the atom was also important.

Another version of the S.S. Clermont *is depicted here. The artist had evidently not seen the real* Clermont *of Robert Fulton (shown above) and portrayed one as seen in his or her mind's eye, sailing in a peaceful, rural setting.*

French chemist Louis Pasteur (1822-1895), inventor of the pasteurization process, used knowledge obtained in the study of atoms to improve medical technology.

The knowledge of atoms and how they form compounds enabled chemists to separate metals and create stronger, lighter forms of steel. Without this steel, no steamship or locomotive could have been built large enough to carry its own coal supply.

In the field of medicine, the work of people like Louis Pasteur would also have been impossible without knowledge of the atom. Pasteur discovered that microscopic organisms, like yeast, bacteria, and viruses, cause chemical reactions. His study of these microbes allowed Pasteur to invent the processes of pasteurization and vaccination.

Every walk of life was affected by the chemical revolution. Fertilizers for farming, dyes for clothing, perfumes for cosmetics, medicines and tonics for health would not have been possible without the new understanding of atoms. Even the soda fountain owes its existence to chemists who developed ways to separate and compress carbon dioxide gas.

This was the first atomic revolution. It was a chemical revolution that began when the atom became the basis for modern chemistry. New applications of this chemistry continue to enrich our world almost daily. Chemists are in the forefront of industry and technology, experimenting with new medicines, fertilizers, pest controls, plastics, and building materials. Besides these contributions to the modern way of life, the atomic revolution of the nineteenth century set the stage for the second atomic revolution, which started at the beginning of the twentieth century.

What Are Atoms Made Of?

The question, "What are atoms made of?" would have seemed silly to most nineteenth-century scientists. When they spoke of atoms, they pictured extremely small, solid particles. They thought of the atom as absolutely the smallest particle in the world. The idea that an atom is made up of even smaller parts seemed preposterous.

Yet a series of discoveries near the turn of the century, most of which were accidental, changed this understanding. These discoveries revealed that at least some atoms give off energy as well as particles smaller than the atom itself. By the year 1900, many scientists were asking in bewilderment, "What *is* the atom made of?"

The Electron Is Discovered

One of the inventions that made subatomic particle research possible was the Crookes Tube. Invented in 1894 by Sir William Crookes, an English physicist, this glass tube was specially designed for studying electricity. It is an airtight glass tube with metal wires at either end. All the air is pumped out of the tube so that there is a complete vacuum, or absence of air, inside. The wire on one end has a negative electrical charge. It is called a cathode. The wire on the other end, called an anode, normally has no electrical charge.

When the anode is given a positive charge, a softly glowing ray of light arcs

English physicist Sir William Crookes (1832-1919) invented the first cathode ray tube. Also called the Crookes Tube, it produced an electrical arc out of electrons, thus showing scientists that atoms were made up of even smaller particles.

across the tube between the cathode and the anode. This light is electricity, which Crookes defined as a stream of negatively charged particles, called electrons, that flow from a negatively charged post to a positive one. From this instrument came some of the first hints of the atom's potential as a source of energy.

A year after the Crookes Tube was invented, Professor J. J. Thomson, of

CROOKES TUBE AND THE DISCOVERY OF THE ELECTRON

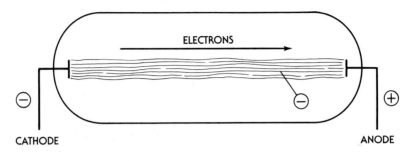

CATHODE ⊖   ELECTRONS ⊖   ⊕ ANODE

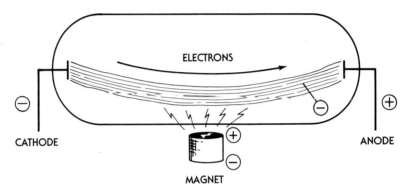

CATHODE ⊖   ELECTRONS ⊖   ⊕ ANODE

MAGNET

Crookes Tube is an airtight tube through which electricity, or a stream of electrons, passes from a negatively-charged wire (or cathode) to a positively-charged wire (or anode). In

1895, J. J. Thomson proved that electrons are negatively-charged particles by showing how the stream of electrons can be bent by the positive pole of a magnet.

Cavendish Institute at Cambridge University in England, proved that electrons are parts of atoms. First he held the positive end of a magnet near the Crookes Tube. The ray of electrons arched in the direction of the magnet. His experiment showed that electrons are particles, and that a single electron weighs far less than a hydrogen atom. Despite their diminutive size, each electron carries a negative electrical charge equal in strength to the positive charge of one positively charged hydrogen atom.

Thomson reasoned that since the hydrogen atom is the lightest of all atoms, and electrons are only a tiny fraction of the size of a hydrogen atom, they must be parts of atoms. The rest of the atom, he believed, must contain enough units of positive charge to balance each of its electrons. Thomson's theories made the chemists' picture of the atom as a small, indestructible piece of matter obsolete. He replaced it with his model of the atom: a positively charged sphere with negative electrons embedded in it. If you can picture a scoop of ice cream with chocolate chips embedded in it, you have a good idea of what Thomson thought the atom looked like.

If electrons are parts of atoms, how do they form streams of electricity? Thomson speculated that a strong positive charge can rip the electrons out of their atoms and send them flying toward the location of the positive charge. That is what happens in a Crookes Tube. Thomson had opened an entirely new field of study, the field that today we call particle physics. A rush of experiments by other physicists and chemists tested his new model of the atom and its subatomic parts.

Becquerel Discovers Radioactivity

One of those obsessed by the mysteries of the atom was the French physicist Henri Becquerel. Quite accidentally, Becquerel discovered yet another form of energy given off by some atoms. He called this energy radioactivity. Becquerel discovered radioactivity while experimenting with a Crookes Tube and a fluorescent screen. This is a screen coated with uranium so that it glows when struck by electrons.

The fluorescent screen in Becquerel's experiment was meant to be a tool for detecting electrons, but he became more intrigued by the tool than by the experiment he was conducting. He noticed that the uranium material seemed to glow not only when struck by electrons but also when left in the sunlight.

So Becquerel began to experiment with the uranium. He wrapped black paper around a few photographic plates and then set several samples of urani-

French physicist Henri Becquerel was obsessed by the mysteries of the atom. He accidentally discovered radioactivity while experimenting with a tool for detecting electrons.

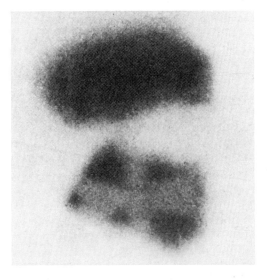

In an 1896 experiment, Becquerel discovered that uranium emitted radiation when he developed this photographic plate and found it had been fogged by exposure to the uranium.

um on top of the paper. After a few days, he developed his photographic plates and found that they had been exposed by the uranium. Some kind of rays, or radiation, were coming directly from the uranium and passing right through the black paper.

Madame Curie's Two New Elements

Where did this radiation come from? Polish scientist Marie Curie was already providing some answers. Like Becquerel, Madame Curie was obsessed by the peculiar behavior of uranium. She managed to convince her physicist husband that the best way to solve the mystery of radioactivity was to buy a ton of uranium ore and experiment with it. For several months, a huge sample of uranium ore sat in the wooden building in the heart of Paris that housed the Curies' home and laboratory.

Ore is a rock that contains metal, in this case, uranium. To use the metal, one must separate it chemically from its ore. So Madame Curie began testing the uranium ore that sat in her home. To her surprise she discovered that the ore, even with all its impurities, was more radioactive than pure uranium.

She concluded that there must be a more radioactive metal than uranium present in the ore, and she set about trying to find it. She removed chunks of lead and other nonradioactive minerals until she was left with a small chunk of highly radioactive material. Not all the material was uranium. Madame Curie discovered a brand new radioactive element, a heavy metal that she named polonium after her native country, Poland. Polonium, with an

Polish scientist Marie Curie broke down a huge sample of uranium ore until she found two elements within it that were even more radioactive than the uranium itself. Her work showed that radioactivivy is a characteristic that distinguishes one element from another.

atomic weight of 239, became element number 94 on the periodic table.

With all the uranium, polonium, and nonradioactive materials removed from the original ore, there was still a tiny piece of rock left. It was so radioactive that it glowed faintly in the dark and gave off so much heat that it was a few degrees warmer than the surrounding air. This turned out to be another new radioactive element, more than two million times more radioactive than pure uranium. Madame Curie called this element radium, which means "the glowing one." Radium, atomic number 88, has an atomic weight of 226.

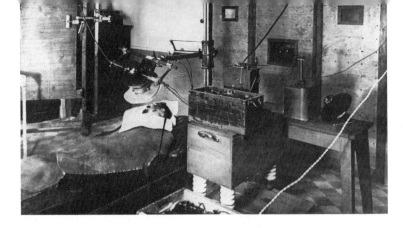

A cancer patient is treated with radium and X-rays in Madame Curie's laboratory shown here at the Radium Institute at the University of Paris in 1928.

Marie Curie's ingenious detective work had turned up two new radioactive elements. More importantly, she showed that radioactivity is a characteristic that distinguishes one element from another. And she showed that this property is almost exclusively a property of the heaviest elements.

During her lifetime, Madame Curie and her husband were awarded two Nobel Prizes for their research on radioactivity. But it cost them dearly. At the time no one knew that radiation can cause cancer. In 1934, at the age of sixty-four, Madame Curie died from what was diagnosed as a rare form of blood poisoning. She may well have been the world's first victim of radioactive poisoning.

J. J. Thomson and other top physicists were fascinated by Madame Curie's findings. The brightest people in the field now applied themselves to figuring out what caused this strange radioactivity. One of the brightest of all was Thomson's young assistant, Ernest Rutherford.

The Divisible Atom

To study radiation, Rutherford and Thomson designed a kind of atomic "gun." It was a hollow block of lead that contained a piece of radium. The rays emitted by the highly radioactive substance could not penetrate the lead box, but they could pass through a small hole in one end of the box. This enabled the scientists to study the rays as they left the box in a steady stream.

At the same time that Rutherford and Thomson were doing their experiments, other scientists tested this stream of radiation with magnets, and they soon found that it was made up of three different kinds of rays. One ray was composed of relatively heavy, positively charged particles. The atomic weight of one of these particles was 4, exactly the same as an atom of helium. These particles became known as alpha particles.

Physicist Ernest Rutherford, pictured here, helped design a method that enabled scientists to further study the cause of radioactivity. In later experiments, he developed a new model for the structure of an atom.

THREE RADIOACTIVE RAYS

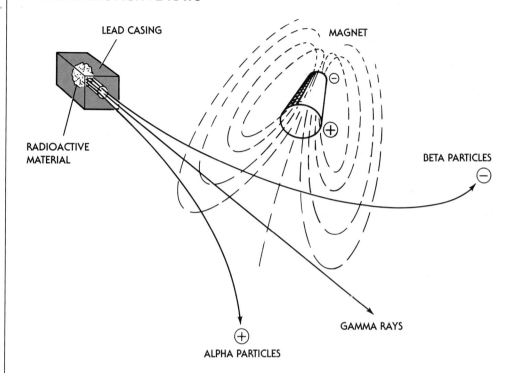

The earliest experiments with radioactive materials showed that they all emit three kinds of rays: alpha, beta, and gamma rays. By testing these three rays with a magnet, scientists found that two of the rays are made up of particles that react to the magnet. Alpha particles are positively charged particles with an atomic weight of 4. Beta particles are identical to electrons. They carry a negative charge and are nearly weightless. The third kind of rays, gamma rays, were unaffected by the magnet. That meant they were either particles with no charge, or a form of energy with no mass.

The second kind of radioactive ray behaved exactly like a stream of electrons. It was made up of tiny, almost weightless negative particles. For the purpose of studying radioactivity, these streams of electrons were called beta particles.

The scientists' primary tool in identifying alpha and beta particles was the magnet. The way it bent the rays helped them determine each particle's weight and electrical charge. On the third kind of radiation, gamma rays, the magnet was of no use. It did not bend these rays at all. Were they made up of neutral particles or were they just energy waves? Gamma rays remained a mystery.

The picture of the atom emerging from the laboratories of physicists was different from the solid, stable spheres pictured by nineteenth-century chemists. Instead of the constant, unchang-

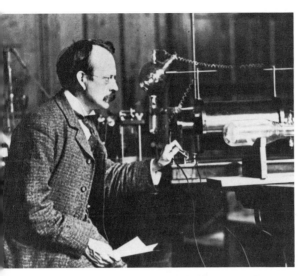

Experiments by physicist J. J. Thomson, shown here in his lab around 1900, contributed to the discovery that atoms of radioactive elements constantly break into smaller pieces and create new atoms.

ing, fundamental building blocks of nature, whose very name means "indivisible," the atoms of radioactive elements, like uranium, radium, and plutonium, are not only divisible, but they also spend their entire existence breaking themselves into smaller pieces and creating new atoms. An entirely new concept of the atom was needed, one that would explain the strange behavior of radioactive elements.

Decaying Atoms

The experiments of Thomson, Rutherford and others showed that the atoms of radioactive elements are constantly getting rid of subatomic parts, the alpha and beta particles seen in their experiments. In this way, an atom of a radioactive element transforms itself into a lighter atom of a different element. Atoms of uranium, for example, change into atoms of radium.

But radium is also radioactive, and its atoms throw out more alpha and beta particles and become atoms of radon, yet another radioactive element. So these, too, continue to change until finally the original uranium atoms are transformed into atoms of lead, which are stable. This process is known as radioactive decay.

Radioactive decay does not happen all at once. The process occurs slowly, over a long period of time. An atom of radium, uranium, or some other radioactive element may exist for years without breaking down. Then, all of a sudden, it will be struck by an alpha, beta, or gamma ray from another atom, and that disturbance will be enough to knock out some of its particles.

Although no one can tell when a particular atom is going to break down, scientists can predict an element's rate of decay with great precision. They measure a radioactive material's rate of decay by its half-life. Radium, for instance, has a half-life of 1,580 years. If you take a block of radium of any size, in 1,580 years only half of that block will still be radium. In the next 1,580 years, another half of it will break down, and so on. This is an extremely short half-life compared to uranium, which has a half-life of over four billion years. That means radium is far more radioactive, or unstable, than uranium.

The discovery of radioactive decay might have made an alchemist from the Middle Ages envious. It appeared to be just the kind of transmutation of elements the alchemists of old had believed possible. To scientists who had just become comfortable with the chemical model of the atom, these findings may have seemed just as shocking as discovering that gold could be changed into lead.

Rutherford Probes the Atom

All this evidence of radioactivity made scientists wonder what really was going on inside the atom. It also gave Ernest Rutherford an idea. The year was 1911, and by then Rutherford had become a professor in Manchester, England. He decided to take his idea of an atomic gun and create an atomic shooting range. He would use alpha particles as "bullets" to probe the atoms of other elements.

Rutherford chose gold as his first subject. His shooting range consisted of a hollow lead block containing a sample of radium, a thin sheet of gold foil, a fluorescent screen, and a microscope. The hole in the lead block was aimed at the gold foil, behind which Rutherford placed the fluorescent screen and the microscope. Alpha particles from the radium shot out of the lead block toward the gold foil. By observing the fluorescent screen through his microscope, Rutherford saw that almost all of the tiny "atomic bullets" passed right through the gold foil as if it were not even there.

Gold, with an atomic weight of 197, is one of the densest metals on earth. And even a thin piece of gold foil is about two thousand atoms thick. So, compared to the tiny alpha particle, the piece of foil was like the Great Wall of China. Yet only about one out of every eight thousand particles fired at the foil was deflected. The rest sailed right through the foil as if they were flying through empty space.

According to Rutherford, that is exactly what they were flying through. He concluded that the inside of an atom is not a positively charged sphere, as Thomson had hypothesized. It is mostly empty space. His experiment also proved that the entire positive charge and more than 99 percent of an atom's weight are packed into an incredibly small, dense particle at the center of the atom. Rutherford named this center the nucleus, and he claimed that an atom's negatively-charged electrons orbit the positive nucleus like a planet orbits the sun.

Rutherford even calculated how far away from the nucleus these electrons had to orbit. Considering how small an atom really is, his conclusion was rather surprising. As his experiments demonstrated, even though the nucleus carries almost all of the atom's weight, it is so small that only one out of every eight thousand alpha particles actually comes close to it. Rutherford estimated that the nucleus must be between ten and fifty thousand times smaller than the atom itself.

To get some idea how small that is, consider the size of the atom itself. Imagine that you were making an "atomic" gold chain, one atom at a time. If you added one atom every second, nonstop, day and night, it would take you eight years to make a chain one inch long. That's how small a whole atom is. The nucleus is ten to fifty thousand times smaller than that, and all the rest of the atom is empty space.

A New Model

This, then, is the model of the atom that Rutherford presented to the world in 1911. A hard, dense nucleus, a particle less than one ten-thousandth of the diameter of the invisible atom, is surrounded by empty space and electrons whirling around it at nearly the speed of light. The negative charge of each min-

RUTHERFORD'S ATOMIC SHOOTING RANGE

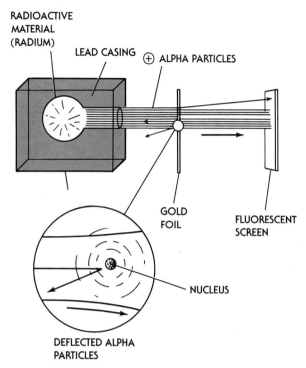

In 1911, Rutherford aimed alpha particles from radioactive radium into a sheet of gold foil. Most of the particles passed directly through the foil and flashed on a fluorescent screen behind it. This proved that most of the volume of an atom had to be empty space. Some of the alpha particles were deflected either partially or completely. Those that bounced straight back were the ones that had been heading directly for the nucleus of an atom. Since they were shot back with such great force, Rutherford concluded that the nucleus of an atom must be an extremely dense, but tiny particle.

ute, practically weightless electron is balanced by a positive unit in the nucleus, claimed Rutherford. He called these positive units protons. The number of negative electrons in an atom is exactly the same as the number of protons.

For example, the first element on the periodic table is hydrogen. It contains only one proton and one electron. The next element on the table is helium. It contains two protons and two electrons. The third element, lithium, contains three protons and three electrons, and so on, with a different element for every number all the way up to 106. The element carbon has 6 protons and 6 electrons, sulfur has 16 and 16, iron 26 and 26, gold 79 and 79, lead has 82 and 82, and uranium, the heaviest element that exists naturally, has 92 protons and 92 electrons.

There are electrons everywhere, including at the surface of objects. These electrons create a solid exterior, much

A young Danish physicist, Niels Bohr, believed he had some important, original insights into the structure of atoms. He approached Rutherford with his ideas.

should lose energy and collapse into the nucleus.

Rutherford could not find the satisfactory answer, but in his typical fashion, he said he did not care. He would leave the theoretical explanations to others. Rutherford was a colorful character with a rather nervous disposition and very little patience. He was a heavyset man who spoke loudly and bluntly, often punctuating his comments with sweeping gestures. He liked to play the role of the simple, unpretentious New Zealand immigrant, who had little interest in abstract theory.

Rutherford's Protégé

There was one theoretical physicist, however, with whom Rutherford became very close, and in whose work he showed a lasting and almost fatherly concern. This was Niels Bohr, the Danish physicist who developed a mathematical theory to explain Rutherford's model of the atom. Both in temperament and style, these two were almost complete opposites, which makes the story of their close friendship interesting. From a purely practical point of view, their friendship had a great impact on science. These two men, Rutherford and Bohr, were the founders of modern nuclear physics.

In 1911, a bashful, twenty-six-year-old Niels Bohr entered Rutherford's office in Manchester. Bohr was tall, thin, and very quiet. It must have taken a great deal of courage for him to approach Rutherford, the rising star of English science. But Bohr had been studying under J. J. Thomson, Rutherford's former teacher, at the Cavendish Institute in Cambridge, and he was very

like the whirling blades of an airplane propeller seem to create a solid shape. Electrons work the same way, but they move thousands of times faster than the fastest propeller. This book that you are holding looks and feels solid. Yet in every millimeter, in the dot of every "i", millions of electrons are whirling madly about.

The work of Rutherford and other physicists in the first decade of the twentieth century shocked the scientific community. It was hard to believe that even the most solid objects are made up almost entirely of empty space. Although there seemed to be no other explanation for Rutherford's experiments, his results seemed to defy the classical laws of physics. According to these laws, the orbits of electrons are impossible. As they revolve around a nucleus, electrons

Bohr's calculations ultimately produced a model of the atom still used today, based on Rutherford's model of orbiting electrons.

unhappy there. He believed that he had made some important, original insights into atomic structure, but he could not get Thomson's interest.

It is a credit to Rutherford's judgment of character that he took the time to listen to the young man. Bohr, even in his later years, was notorious for his long, drawn-out, indirect manner of discussion. And he spoke so softly that he was practically whispering.

Rutherford was never known for his patience or his appreciation for theoreticians. Blunt-spoken, excitable, and sometimes even explosive, he was used to dominating others in a conversation. Yet he must have instinctively recognized Bohr's intelligence, for he listened patiently. Perhaps it is a tribute to his kindness that he saw that the young man was unhappy, and he offered him a position at the university. Seldom has an act of kindness borne such positive results.

Bohr thrived under Rutherford's enthusiastic encouragement. For the next two years, the two men worked together. At the end of that time, Bohr produced the model of the atom that we still use today. It was based on Rutherford's model of orbiting electrons, but Bohr's model made a daring new assertion

Bohr found that electrons held packets of energy in place within atoms, that these packets or quanta come in different sizes and that larger quanta contain more energy.

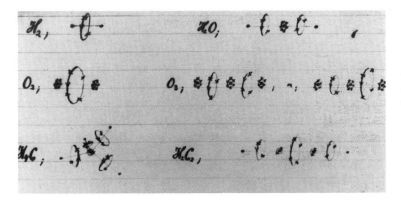

This sketch of atomic structure done by Bohr shows electrons arranged around the atom's nucleus like shells or the layers of an onion. This arrangement determined the physical and chemical properties of all elements and compounds.

that explained how these electrons stay in orbit.

Bohr Defines Electron Orbits

To do so, he made use of an important theory from the German physicist Max Planck. Planck's theory is called the quantum theory. In its simplest terms, it states that light or any other form of energy travels in waves. But these waves are not continuous. Instead, they are divided into incredibly small packets, and each of these packets of energy is called a quantum.

Where do these quanta come from? Planck and Albert Einstein, a German-born American physicist, had both stated that they come from atoms, although they had not explained how. Bohr had the answer, and it was brilliant: When a quantum is not traveling in a straight line in the form of a wave, it is circling an atom in the form of an electron orbit. In other words, electrons hold quanta, or packets of energy, in place within atoms.

Every electron occupies a single quantum. But quanta come in different sizes, and the larger the size the greater the energy they contain. There is nothing random about these sizes, however. Bohr showed that the size of quanta are related to the size of electron orbits in a very systematic way. This system is absolute and unchangeable. It is the same for every atom in the universe. Bohr used the term *shells* to describe the different sizes of quanta because they are arranged around the nucleus like shells or like the layers of an onion.

The smallest quanta, or orbits, are so small that only two of them fit around the nucleus of any single atom. Therefore, no more than two electrons can orbit a nucleus in this shell. If the atom contains more than two electrons, the other electrons must occupy larger quanta. The next shell has room for eight quanta or electrons, as do most of the other shells.

Electron Orbits Determine Chemical Properties

Bohr's arrangement of electrons in shells was an important breakthrough for chemists. At long last they could see that this arrangement of electrons determines the physical and chemical properties of all elements and com-

THE CHANGING PICTURE OF THE ATOM

BEFORE THOMSON

THOMSON 1904

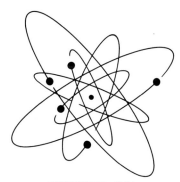

RUTHERFORD 1911

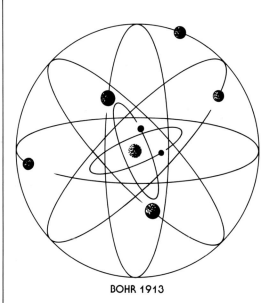

BOHR 1913

From the time John Dalton proposed his theory of the atom in 1803 to the time Niels Bohr defined electron orbits as quanta of energy, scientists' picture of the atom has been constantly changing. Before J. J. Thomson identified electrons as subatomic particles in 1904, the atom was generally pictured as a solid sphere with no electrical charge. Thomson envisioned the atom as a semi-solid sphere with electrons embedded in it. In 1911, Ernest Rutherford proved that the atom was mostly empty space. In his view, the atom had an extremely small, dense, positively-charged nucleus at the core and negatively-charged electrons whirling around it in no particular order. Two years later, Bohr adjusted Rutherford's model of the atom by showing that electrons orbit in specific shells.

pounds. Specifically, the number of electrons in the outermost shell of an atom gives an element its most distinctive characteristics.

The hydrogen atom, for example, has a single electron and a single proton. A helium atom has two protons and two electrons. But that one extra little electron in the helium atom makes all the difference in the world. Its electron shell is filled to the maximum. In this most stable of conditions, an atom has no place for another electron orbit, so it rarely combines with other atoms. For this reason helium is called an inert, or inactive, element.

Hydrogen, on the other hand, is extremely active. It has just one electron

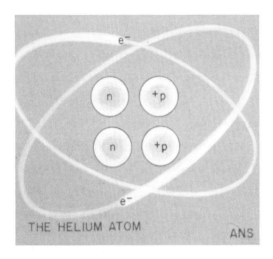

THE HELIUM ATOM

ANS

Helium atoms, like this one, have two protons and two electrons. Because helium rarely combines with other atoms, it is called an inert or inactive element.

in its shell, so it has room for another electron. Or it may combine with another atom that has seven electrons in its outer shell, like chlorine. This will fill up the chlorine atom's outer shell with eight electrons, forming the stable compound hydrogen chloride (HCl).

Pure hydrogen gas also appears abundantly in the atmosphere. That is because two hydrogen atoms can combine to share electrons and form a stable molecule (H_2). These molecules of hydrogen gas are also active. They combine with atoms like oxygen, which need two additional electrons to fill their outer shell. The result of this combination is, of course, H_2O, or water.

Ever since Mendeleev invented the periodic table in 1863, chemists had relied on it to predict the chemical behavior of elements. Perhaps the most remarkable thing about this table is that it was developed without Bohr's model of the atom. In 1863, Mendeleev assigned every known element an atom-ic number. It was simply based on arranging the elements by atomic weight. Hydrogen, for example, had the atomic number 1, because it was the lightest of all elements. Helium was number 2, lithium 3, and so on.

Fifty years later, Bohr found the secret behind the periodic table. He discovered that the atomic numbers tell exactly how many electrons and how many protons are in each atom of a given element. The atomic number for carbon, for example, is 6. This means an atom of carbon has 6 electrons and 6 protons. Oxygen, with atomic number 8, has 8 electrons and 8 protons in each atom. Iron, number 26, has 26 electrons and protons.

Now for the first time, chemists could understand why physical and chemical characteristics were repeated every eight elements. The electrons in the outermost shell of an atom give it most of its physical features. Most electron shells hold a maximum of eight electrons, and when one shell is filled, a new shell is started.

By 1920, the picture of the atom developed by Rutherford and Bohr had revolutionized the study of chemistry and physics. With the knowledge of electron bonding, chemists understood how molecules were formed. They could finally see how the minuscule atom and its arrangement of electrons cause the tremendous variety of matter. While the effects of electrons became increasingly evident, however, there was still little known about the mass of the atom and its well-protected nucleus. Understanding electrons had unlocked the chemical secrets of the atom, but the atom's power remained hidden in its mysterious nucleus.

The Missing Piece

Shortly after Niels Bohr published his quantum theory of the atom, he became a celebrated figure. In his native Denmark, Bohr was a national hero, and the nation wanted its hero to return home. Bohr was reluctant to leave Manchester, where his work with Rutherford had been both enjoyable and productive. They made a fine team, Bohr the theorist and Rutherford the experimenter. Bohr was indebted to his friend for giving him a chance to prove himself and to develop his theories. But Rutherford had been well-rewarded, for Bohr's theory was a victory for Rutherford's model of the atom, too.

Bohr's Institute of Theoretical Physics

Soon the Danes made it impossible for Bohr to resist their invitations. They not only offered him a position, they offered him his own institute. The Institute for Theoretical Physics in Copenhagen was designed for him and by him. It was a center unlike any other in the history of physics. Its laboratories were equipped with the finest microscopes, scales, and other equipment. And with Bohr as its director, it became a gathering place for scientists from around the world.

Bohr was only in his midthirties when he assumed the directorship of the new institute. But renowned scientists from around the world now traveled to Copenhagen to hear him talk, which he did at considerable length. His discussions—slow, contemplative, and full of seemingly irrelevant side trips—always seemed to wind their way toward provocative understanding and revelation.

From the outset, Ernest Rutherford had urged his friend to accept the position in Copenhagen. It might have been generosity that inspired him, or it may have been foresight. J. J. Thomson would soon be retiring from the Cavendish Institute, and in 1919, Rutherford would take his place as the prestigious director of that research facility.

As the directors of the world's two foremost physics institutes, Bohr and Rutherford continued to benefit from their friendship. Reflecting the influence of their directors, the two schools complemented one another well, and they were set to lead the new atomic physics revolution. At Cavendish, Rutherford continued to probe the atom with alpha particles. As a rule the Cavendish school made the new discoveries, and the Copenhagen school developed the mathematical principles to explain them.

The Copenhagen school became a hallmark of theory, as Bohr gathered around him many of the best mathematical minds in the world. The most important theory they developed became known as quantum mechanics. These were the mathematical formulae for determining the size and amounts of energy represented by the quanta of all atoms.

Einstein and Quantum Mechanics

Quantum mechanics received an important assist from an unexpected source. Albert Einstein, the most celebrated scientist alive, was at that time serving on the faculty of the University of Zurich in Switzerland.

He was a gentle person, who worked in a uniquely independent way. He did not need the stimulation of a busy laboratory filled with assistants. In fact, he performed very few experiments. Einstein once wrote that he admired Rutherford's gift for experimentation and wished that he could think of such experiments himself.

Physicist Albert Einstein, pictured in this portrait, had a unique ability to mentally focus on and work through extremely complex ideas. Einstein later received a Nobel Prize for his work on atomic structure.

Instead, most of his experiments were what he called thought experiments, a kind of imaginary experiment. This was his particular gift. What separated Einstein from other scientists of this century, perhaps of any century, was his ability to mentally focus on and work through extremely complex ideas. For hours on end, he could focus on these thought experiments, sustaining and remembering all the twists and turns in his mental route through the experiment toward the correct result.

Einstein did not have a great interest in the atom. His real interest was in space, the cosmos, the arrangement of the universe. In later years, scientists began to realize that his special theory of relativity applied as strongly to the world of subatomic particles as it did to space, but Einstein himself did surprisingly little work on atomic structure.

It is ironic, then, that Einstein's Nobel Prize was awarded for his contribution in this area and not for his theories of relativity. Specifically, his prize was awarded for his contributions to quantum mechanics. As early as 1905, when Einstein was still in his twenties, he had shown that light is made up of waves and quanta. He had demonstrated that quanta of light are somehow given off by "excited" electrons. Einstein called these quanta of light photons, and he referred to the phenomenon of light as the photoelectric effect. But he did not know how it was generated.

When he read about Bohr's atom in 1913, he declared, "This is one of the greatest discoveries ever." Immediately, he saw the connection to his own theory of the photoelectric effect. An excited electron is one that changes orbits. It becomes excited by absorbing a quantum of energy.

HOW PHOTONS CAUSE LIGHT

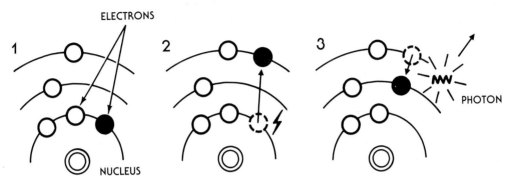

Atoms give off light when they are "excited" by an outside energy source, such as heat or light. A beam of light is a form of electromagnetic energy. Electromagnetic energy is composed of billions of photons, or tiny bursts of energy, that travel in waves. The diagram above shows how atoms emit photons.

1.   Every atom contains electrons that revolve around its nucleus in various orbits, or energy levels. The level closest to the nucleus is the lowest energy level, and the one farthest from the nucleus is the highest.

2.   When an atom is "excited" by an external energy source, at least one of its electrons picks up extra energy and jumps to the highest energy level.

3.   An electron that has jumped to the highest level will soon return to a lower level. When it does, it rids itself of the extra energy. That energy is emitted as a photon.

How Electrons Produce Light

It is the very nature of an electron to absorb energy. That's what an electron is—nature's quantum absorber. When it occupies a quantum, it keeps the quantum orbiting around a nucleus. A quantum then has two possible forms. It can radiate, or travel as a wave, or it can stop radiating and serve as an electron orbit. Electrons are like little light switches. When they absorb a quantum they "turn off" its radiation, and when they give up a quantum they turn the light, or radiation, back on.

How does an electron give up a quantum? Inside the atom an excited electron may jump from a smaller orbit or quantum to a larger one. But as we have seen, elements naturally fill their inner shells, or lower levels of energy, before they occupy larger quanta. So the excited electron is really out of place. It has vacated a smaller quantum for a larger one. Soon the pull of the positively charged nucleus will draw the negatively charged electron back to its proper inner shell, and the electron must let go of the bigger quantum. The released quantum then shoots out of the atom as a photon, or light wave.

Using Bohr's arrangement of quanta, Einstein worked out the exact wavelengths of light that one could expect to be released from the various electron shells. At the Copenhagen Institute, scientists used extremely sensitive light meters to test Einstein's predictions. They matched perfectly.

Einstein's so-called photoelectric effect explained why electrons do not lose energy and collapse into the nucleus. An electron keeps the quantum in a steady, stable orbit. And centrifugal force, the same force that keeps planets moving on stable orbits around the sun, keeps electrons moving in their orbits.

Einstein had relied heavily on the theories and formulas of quantum mechanics created by Max Planck and developed by Bohr's Copenhagen Institute. On one important principle, however, Einstein and Bohr disagreed. This principle of quantum theory is known as the uncertainty principle, which holds that the location of a particular electron at any given moment is completely unpredictable. Electrons move so fast and have so little mass that their orbits are impossible to track.

Although this principle has since been proven true, its greatest historical significance is that Einstein disagreed with it. His disagreement with Bohr over the uncertainty principle became so highly publicized that even today it obscures the far more important ways in which the theories of Einstein and Bohr helped to change the modern understanding of so many things, including light.

Rutherford Finds the Proton

One person who had little use for the public squabble over the uncertainty principle was Ernest Rutherford. Rutherford was too interested in experiments, in gathering new facts and making new revelations about atoms to spend much time analyzing or theorizing about them. He worked closely with his friend, Niels Bohr, and referred gruffly to Einstein and the other theoretical physicists as "those theory fellows." At the Cavendish Institute, Rutherford gathered the finest group of experimental physicists in the world, and together they continued to probe the atom, leaving the theoretical interpretation to "those fellows."

His original atomic probes were of gold. But in 1919, Rutherford began to fire alpha particles at nitrogen atoms instead. He managed to knock something from the nucleus of nitrogen that resembled the nucleus of a hydrogen atom. As a result, the nitrogen atom had been converted into oxygen.

Rutherford was most intrigued, however, by the particle that had been knocked loose from the nitrogen nucleus. It had a positive charge of one unit, exactly the same as a hydrogen nucleus. And it weighed exactly the same as a hydrogen atom, also one atomic unit. This particle had not come from a hydrogen atom, however, but from a nitrogen atom.

Rutherford concluded that he had isolated the proton, the fundamental unit that gives nuclei their positive charge. Since the proton is identical to a hydrogen nucleus, which has a single positive charge, then a helium nucleus must contain two protons, a lithium nucleus three protons, and so on. For every electron, there is one proton.

The results of this experiment fit the Rutherford-Bohr model of the atom, with one important exception. The atomic weights of all the elements except hydrogen were about twice as heavy as they should have been. A single proton accounted for all the weight in the hydrogen atom, but in all the other elements, the protons accounted for only about half of the atom's weight.

There must have been something else inside the nuclei of these atoms that weighed about as much as all its protons. After he had isolated the proton in 1919, Rutherford predicted that another particle would someday be found inside the nucleus of an atom. He predicted that the particle would weigh about the same as a proton but would have no electrical charge.

The Neutron Is Discovered

In 1932, James Chadwick, one of Rutherford's faculty members at the Cavendish Institute, was experimenting with the radioactive element beryllium. He bombarded beryllium samples with alpha particles, just as Rutherford had done to gold and nitrogen. Chadwick noticed that a few of these alpha particles knocked unidentified particles out of the beryllium nuclei. When these particles shot out of their atoms, they began knocking protons out of other beryllium nuclei.

Chadwick tested these unidentified particles with a magnet. They were unaffected, meaning they had no charge. They had to be at least the size of a proton or they would not have been able to knock protons out of their nuclei. Chadwick had discovered the neutral particles that his professor had predicted. He named them neutrons.

Finally the picture of the atom seemed complete. The nucleus contains positively-charged protons and neutrons with no charge. Together they make up the total weight of the atom. Surrounding the nucleus are layers of whirling electrons, with one negatively-charged electron in orbit around the nucleus to balance each proton inside.

The Power of the Neutron

The discovery of the neutron in 1932 set off an intense wave of scientific activity. Scientists soon found that the neutron made an excellent new bullet for probing atoms. Since the neutron has no charge, it is often a better atomic bullet than an alpha particle. For one thing, the neutron is not repelled by a nucleus the way an alpha particle would be. Instead, the neutron can keep on going, right into the heart of the nucleus.

Probing the Atom with Neutrons

One of the first to probe the atom with neutrons was the Italian physicist Enrico Fermi. At the University of Rome in 1932, Fermi adopted Rutherford's method of probing nuclei, but instead of shooting alpha particles into the nuclei, he used neutrons.

Fermi developed the world's first neutron "gun," a glass tube no more than one-half inch long. Inside this tube were small quantities of radium and beryllium. The radium shot alpha particles that knocked free neutrons from the beryllium. And the neutrons were aimed at samples of uranium.

The experiments of Fermi and his colleagues convinced them that neutrons possessed a force entirely different from all other known forces. They called it the nuclear force, and they concluded that it is what holds a nucle-

Italian physicist Enrico Fermi was one of the first scientists to probe the atom with neutrons. Although he did not know it at the time, he was the first scientist to split the atom in two. This process is called fission.

us together. Inside the densely packed nucleus of an atom, neutrons exert a tremendously powerful attraction for other neutrons and for protons. This attraction is so strong that it holds protons together with neutrons, despite the powerful force of repulsion between protons.

But the neutron's job of keeping a nucleus stable grows more difficult as the atoms get heavier. The increasing number of protons create an enormous amount of repulsion, so extra neutrons are needed. Atoms with less than 20 protons require only one neutron for each proton. An atom of helium, for example, contains 2 protons and 2 neutrons. Therefore its atomic weight is 4. Carbon, with an atomic weight of 12, has 6 protons and 6 neutrons. Oxygen, atomic weight 16, has 8 of each.

When an atomic nucleus contains more than 20 protons, it needs more than an equal number of neutrons to

hold the nucleus together. An iron atom, for example, has 26 protons, but it requires at least 28 neutrons to stabilize it. The tin atom, which contains 50 protons in its nucleus, needs at least 62 neutrons to keep it stable. Lead, with its 82 protons, normally contains 126 neutrons in its nucleus, or 44 more neutrons than protons. All these extra neutrons are needed to keep the 82 protons from flying out of the nucleus.

Most elements have atoms with slightly different atomic weights. That is because some have more neutrons in the nucleus than others. Atoms of the same element with different atomic weights are called isotopes. Iron, for example, can be found in four different isotopes—one with 28 neutrons, another with 30, still another with 31, and even one with 32 neutrons. Even the simplest elements have different isotopes. Most hydrogen atoms, for example, contain no neutrons, but a small percentage of them contain a single neutron. With an atomic weight of 2 instead of 1, this isotope of hydrogen is called deuterium, or heavy hydrogen. There is even an isotope of ultraheavy hydrogen. With an atomic weight of 3, its nucleus contains two neutrons.

Unstable Atoms

Some elements have no stable isotopes at all, only unstable isotopes. These are the elements that we call radioactive. When the number of protons in a nucleus is over 83, no number of neutrons is enough to hold the nucleus together forever. With protons and neutrons piled closely together in these nuclei, the force of repulsion between two or more protons eventually drives some of these particles out with great force.

HOW A RADIOACTIVE ELEMENT CHANGES

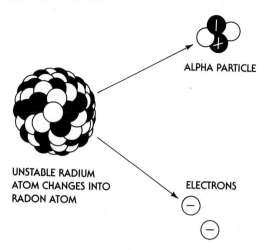

ALPHA PARTICLE

UNSTABLE RADIUM
ATOM CHANGES INTO
RADON ATOM

ELECTRONS

Whenever radium exists, it has come from atoms of uranium that have gradually changed into atoms of radium. But radium is even more radioactive, or unstable, than uranium. Gradually, it changes into a radioactive gas called radon. Radium has an atomic number of 88, meaning it contains 88 protons and 88 electrons. An average of 138 neutrons in the nucleus try to hold its 88 protons together. Occasionally, an alpha particle (with two protons and two neutrons) escapes from the radium nucleus. With its positive charge reduced by two units, the atom soon loses two negatively charged electrons. Now it has become an atom of the radioactive gas radon, with 86 protons and 86 electrons.

When this happens, the tremendous energy required to hold two or more protons together is suddenly released in the form of gamma rays. We call this release of energy nuclear energy.

The particles driven out of a nucleus by radioactive decay are alpha and beta particles. You may recall that an alpha particle has an atomic weight of 4 and a positive charge equal to two protons. That is because these particles are small bundles containing two protons and two neutrons. The nuclear force, or attraction, in this unit is so strong that even when it is knocked out of an unstable nucleus, these four particles stick together as a single alpha particle.

The most puzzling particle of radiation is the beta particle. Like alpha particles, they are emitted from the nucleus of a radioactive atom. But beta particles are electrons, and there are no electrons in the nucleus of an atom. Scientists still do not agree about why this happens.

The most frequently accepted theory was first proposed by Fermi. He maintained that a neutron is an unstable pairing of one proton and one electron. Within the nucleus of an element, even of a stable element, neutrons are constantly emitting their protons and attracting new ones. In a radioactive nucleus, a neutron may lose its proton

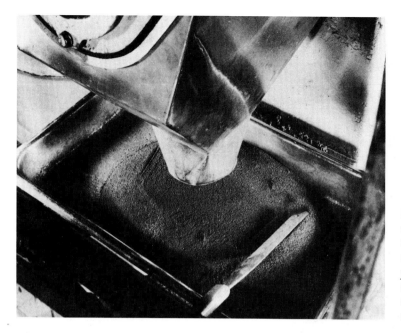

Uranium dioxide powder is mixed, granulated (as shown here) and then compacted into fuel pellets in a principal step in the fabrication of fuel elements for water-cooled reactors.

and not be able to attract a new one. This leaves a lone electron, which is thrown out of the nucleus.

An "Explosion" No One Noticed

In 1934, Fermi and his team of researchers at the University of Rome attempted a new experiment. One of Fermi's greatest gifts was his common sense approach to science. He believed that the neutrons used to bombard uranium atoms would be more likely to stick inside the uranium nuclei if they were moving slower. So he decided to slow them down by shooting them through paraffin wax.

In this way, he expected to load several uranium nuclei and produce highly radioactive isotopes of uranium. Instead, something happened that was entirely unexpected. The nucleus of one uranium atom had absorbed more neutrons than it could manage. Instead

of creating a new element heavier than uranium, the nucleus split into two parts. Instantly the splitting of a single uranium nucleus released thousands of times more energy than the radiation normally produced by a radioactive atom.

In addition, the splitting of the uranium atom produced a peculiar mixture of radioactive elements, including barium and krypton. Each of these elements had atomic weights that were just a little more or a little less than half the atomic weight of uranium. These results were so entirely unexpected that Fermi did not understand their implication. As brilliant a scientist as Fermi was, he did not realize what he had just accomplished. He had been the first person in the world to split the atom in two, and he missed it.

Today we call this process fission. It is used every day in nuclear power plants. But in 1934, all the most respected physicists in the world, including Einstein, Rutherford and Bohr, believed that splitting the atom was impossible.

Otto Hahn, a German chemist pictured here, and Fritz Strassman believed they had split a uranium atom in two although it contradicted the predictions of the world's leading physicists.

The Atom Splits Again, and Again

In 1938, in the German city of Berlin, two chemists, Otto Hahn and Fritz Strassman, decided to repeat Fermi's experiment. They had read articles in which Fermi described the experiment as a failed attempt to produce highly radioactive isotopes of uranium. They were curious about this experiment and wanted to see if they would get the same results as Fermi.

Hahn and Strassman repeated the experiment several times, each time producing barium and krypton. These two chemists, however, noticed the sudden burst of energy released by their experiment. Although they knew it sounded preposterous, they believed

they had split a uranium atom in two. It contradicted the predictions of Rutherford, Bohr, Einstein, Planck, Fermi, and all other leading physicists in the world.

Hahn and Strassman also knew that if splitting the atom were possible, the fission of just a small amount of matter would release an enormous amount of energy. This could potentially be used to build an extremely powerful weapon. Hitler was in power in Germany at the time, and he had recently invaded Austria. Whether they feared that this information might get into the wrong hands in this turbulent time, or just feared the humiliation of being proved wrong, Hahn and Strassman decided not to publish their conclusion.

Instead, their detailed scientific report of the experiment ended with one of the strangest passages in the annals of science. They "could only report as chemists," said their report, that they had unmistakably produced barium and krypton from uranium. "However," they added, "as nuclear chemists, closely allied to physics, we cannot make this jump, so contradictory to all the phenomena observed until now in nuclear physics. . . . It is possible," they concluded, "that a number of rare accidents may have fooled us into making erroneous observations."

Fission Is for Real

Until 1938, Otto Hahn had worked with a research partner named Lise Meitner. Meitner was Jewish and in Hitler's Germany, being Jewish was becoming increasingly dangerous. In the spring of 1938, Meitner escaped to Sweden.

In December she received a letter from Otto Hahn in which he explained

NUCLEAR FUSION

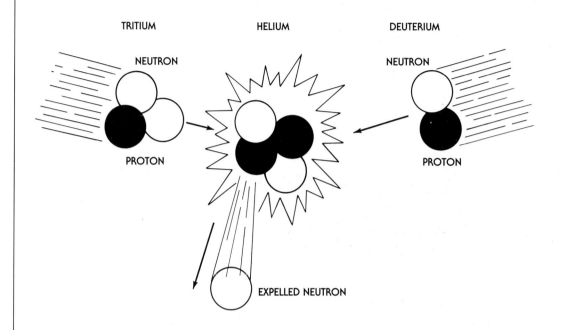

TRITIUM   HELIUM   DEUTERIUM

NEUTRON   NEUTRON

PROTON   PROTON

EXPELLED NEUTRON

Nuclear fusion requires two types, or isotopes, of hydrogen. One of these isotopes is deuterium, which has a single neutron and proton in its nucleus. The other is tritium, which has two neutrons and a proton in its nucleus. When an atom of deuterium and an atom of tritium collide at extremely high temperatures, two protons and two neutrons fuse together to form a nucleus of helium. An extra neutron is expelled from this nucleus with great force. This is the source of energy in the fusion reaction.

his experiment in detail. He also confided his secret belief that he had succeeded in splitting the atom. It so happened that Meitner was entertaining her nephew, Otto Frisch, for Christmas. Frisch was also a physicist who had escaped from Germany and taken refuge in Copenhagen. There he worked with Bohr at the Institute for Theoretical Physics.

The first thing Meitner did when Frisch arrived at her home in Goteberg, Sweden, was show him Hahn's letter. The two of them went for a long walk in the woods. Years later, recalling the moment when he first heard that a uranium nucleus had been split, Frisch said, "I refused to believe the atom could be split. All experience and theory showed that even unstable nuclei do not break up. They simply emit fragments until they become stable."

Meitner would not give up. She knew Hahn too well to believe he could

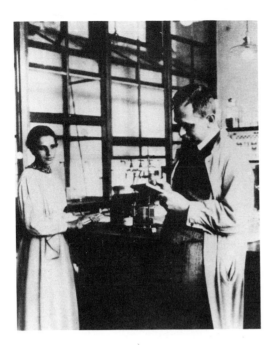

Hahn and research partner Lise Meitner, at work in their lab in 1913, had no idea that Hahn later would split a uranium atom. Meitner independently confirmed Hahn's discoveries.

have repeated the same mistakes unknowingly on several occasions. Finally she convinced Frisch to at least consider the possibility that Hahn was right. The two returned to her home and went to work. They examined Hahn's figures, reviewing his description of the experiment, and searching for an explanation.

Time and again they arrived at the same conclusion. The nucleus of a uranium atom contains 92 protons. Barium contains 56 protons and krypton has 36. The neutrons fired into the uranium nuclei had pushed these heavy nuclei over the brink. But they did not just knock off small fragments or particles. They split in two, with 56 of the protons going into one new atom of barium and 36 into a new atom of krypton, accounting for all 92 protons.

Ninety-two protons suddenly breaking away from each other releases the energy that holds them together. Most of this energy of nuclear fission goes out in the form of powerful gamma rays.

The splitting of the uranium atom signaled the dawn of the atomic age. It opened to humankind both the promise and the terror of the most powerful form of energy ever created by humans. Civilization stood at a crossroads. One way led to a lasting source of power and a more comfortable way of life; the other way led to annihilation. This was a perilous time to be at these crossroads, for World War II was just about to begin.

CHAPTER 5

The Power of Good and Evil

The 1930s was a period of tremendous upheaval in Europe, where most work in atomic physics was taking place. Behind most of this upheaval stood Adolf Hitler. In 1933, Hitler became dictator of Germany, and in 1939, World War II began. The anti-Semitism that Hitler unleashed caused a great emigration of intellectuals from central Europe. The emigrants were not all Jewish people but included many who sympathized with them or who risked their lives by refusing to support the Nazi regime.

Several European scientists took teaching positions at New York City's Columbia University, shown here, after fleeing Adolf Hitler's domination.

The anti-Semitism imposed by Adolf Hitler, pictured here, prompted many intellectuals— some Jewish, some not—to leave central Europe.

The United States, as the richest country and also the most secure from Nazi Germany, received the greatest number of emigrants. Among those who came to the U.S. was Albert Einstein, a pacifist who had spoken out strongly against the persecution of the Jews. Einstein accepted a position at Princeton University in New Jersey.

Columbia University in New York City also benefited greatly from this intellectual windfall. Among the best-known scientists who came to teach and research at Columbia were Enrico Fermi, an Italian, Victor Weisskopf, a German, and Eugene Wigner, Edward Teller, and Leo Szilard, all Hungarian.

A Chain Reaction

Before the war was over, many of these refugee physicists would play a key role in its outcome. Among the first to become involved was Leo Szilard, a professor at Columbia University. He did this by calculating the requirements for a nuclear chain reaction. Until he made his calculations, no one was certain how much uranium would be needed to start a chain reaction, or if one was really possible.

The splitting of a single uranium nucleus releases a considerable amount of energy for such a small particle, but the only way it can really produce significant amounts of energy is by starting a chain reaction. When a nucleus splits, it not only releases energy but also a few neutrons. Many scientists had speculated that these neutrons would penetrate other uranium nuclei and split them. From those splits, more neutrons would be released, and these would split even more nuclei. In other words, splitting one uranium nucleus could start a chain reaction, splitting first one nucleus, then two, then four, then eight, sixteen, thirty-two, and so on. In no time at all, this chain reaction could split millions and billions of uranium atoms, producing a source of energy more powerful than anything the world had ever seen.

However, not every free neutron in a mass of uranium will cause another atom to split. In fact, most free neutrons are simply absorbed by other nu-

Physicist Leo Szilard calculated the requirements for a nuclear chain reaction. He was one of many refugee physicists whose discoveries played a key role in the outcome of World War II.

clei. Others escape from the mass of uranium entirely. A chain reaction of uranium—or any other radioactive material—is possible only if the mass of material is large enough to insure that at least two neutrons from every split atom will contact and split other atoms. Otherwise the chain reaction can never get started. Scientists refer to the minimum mass necessary to start a chain reaction as the "critical mass."

Until March 3, 1939, no one knew what the critical mass of uranium was. Many physicists believed that it was unrealistically large. But on that March day in 1939, Leo Szilard, a professor at Columbia University, calculated that the critical mass of uranium 238, a highly unstable form of uranium, is only about one kilogram (2.2 pounds). According to his calculations, a nuclear chain reaction would be easy to trigger.

A FISSION CHAIN REACTION

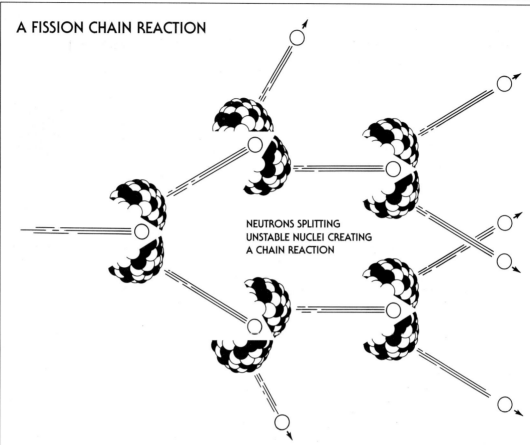

NEUTRONS SPLITTING
UNSTABLE NUCLEI CREATING
A CHAIN REACTION

Fission is a much more explosive change in a radioactive atom than radiation. Fission occurs when a neutron splits a nucleus in two, forcing a heavy radioactive atom to become two atoms of entirely different substances. When the atom splits, it releases a tremendous amount of energy for its size. It also releases a few neutrons, which may fly off and split other nuclei. If two or more of these neutrons split other nuclei, and two or more neutrons from each other of those nuclei split other nuclei, a chain reaction is started. In no time at all, millions of atoms are exploding apart, creating an enormous blast.

The Patriotic Immigrants

Szilard realized that the vast energy released in such a chain reaction could be used in an atomic bomb with a destructive force of millions of times greater than a conventional bomb. He knew that physicists in Germany, where Hahn and Strassman had successfully produced a fission reaction, were trying to develop an atomic bomb, and he believed that Americans should be doing the same.

As a recent immigrant, however, he did not believe that anyone in the United States government would listen to him. Szilard spoke to his colleagues at

Columbia, especially the other emigrant scientists—Fermi, Wigner, Teller, and Weisskopf. They all agreed that the United States had to do something, but they knew only one person who they believed would be heard, Einstein.

When approached with helping the group, however, Einstein, an outspoken pacifist, declined. He did not want to work on developing the most destructive weapon ever conceived. The other scientists agreed to try something else.

Although Fermi was the newest immigrant among this group, he soon became their leader. In April, armed with a letter of introduction from a dean at Columbia University, Fermi headed for Washington, D.C. to visit the Chief of Naval Operations. As far as we know, he was never allowed to see the admiral. Instead, he was met by two young lieutenants who clearly had never heard of Fermi or of fission. In his broken English, Fermi tried to explain to them how a controlled chain reaction of uranium 238 could be used to power atomic submarines and how an uncontrolled chain reaction could make possible atomic bombs millions of times more powerful than any known explosive.

The two young officers listened politely to Fermi, and when he was finished, they asked to be kept informed of any further developments. But no sooner had Fermi left them when one of the officers reportedly said to the other, "That [man] is crazy."

That is where the issue stood for several months. Fermi and his colleagues, who have since become known as the "Fermi Five," discussed among themselves the technology required to produce an atomic bomb. But without funding, they could do little to test their theories.

Hungarian physicist Edward Teller was among the group of refugee scientists at Columbia University who tried to convince the United States government that Germany was developing an atomic bomb and that the U.S. should do the same.

In the summer of 1939, news came that Germany had occupied Czechoslovakia, the country known to have the largest deposits of quality uranium ore in the world. Hitler had immediately confiscated all uranium mining operations. The Fermi Five guessed what this meant.

A Famous Letter

The five decided to go back to Einstein, urging him to speak directly to President Franklin Roosevelt about the need for an American effort to build an atomic bomb. Einstein listened attentively, but sadly. The man who had risked his life in Germany during World War I to express his opposition to war was now being asked to support the building of the most destructive weapon ever conceived by science. Reluctantly, Einstein agreed to sign a letter composed by the group warning the president that the first nation to develop an atomic bomb could virtually hold the rest of the world hostage.

President Franklin Roosevelt received two letters that convinced him to fund atomic bomb research, although funding was minimal until several years later.

On October 11, 1939, the letter was personally taken to President Roosevelt and read to him by Alexander Sachs, a Russian-born colleague of Einstein's. According to popular legend, Einstein's letter is what finally persuaded the U.S. government to pour unlimited funding into the research and development of the atomic bomb. In fact, it probably was not.

A Second Letter

We do know that the letter prompted Roosevelt to appoint a committee to look into the matter. However, more than two agonizing years passed before the president decided to build the bomb. By then, many other factors contributed to the decision. For one thing, Einstein sent President Roosevelt another letter in March 1940. In it he wrote:

> Since the outbreak of the war, interest in uranium has intensified in Germany. I have now learned that research

there is being carried out in great secrecy and that it has been extended to another of the Kaiser Wilhelm Institutes, the Institute of Physics.

In response to Einstein's second letter, the War Department issued the meager sum of six thousand dollars to Columbia University for research on the atomic bomb. With the money, Fermi bought materials to build a graphite "furnace" in which to perform a chain reaction. Over the next two years, the project continued to receive low-level funding from the War Department.

The Chicago Fire That No One Heard About

Early in 1942, the entire graphite-uranium contraption was moved to the University of Chicago, along with Fermi and his team. There the secret project

Enrico Fermi built a graphite furnace, like this one, for conducting experiments that would lead to construction of the first atomic bomb. The primitive furnace was the world's first nuclear reactor.

Fermi's team of scientists ignited the world's first nuclear chain reaction on December 2, 1942, at a test site on the University of Chicago campus, pictured here as it looked during World War II.

was given the code name, "the Metallurgical Laboratory." On December 2, 1942, in the gloomy basement beneath the stands of Stagg Field on the University of Chicago campus, Fermi's team ignited the world's first atomic fire, a nuclear chain reaction that burned for twenty-eight minutes. Then the physicists stopped the chain reaction by using rods of cadmium and boron. These control rods stop an atomic fire like water stops an ordinary fire. For the first time, humans had released the energy of the atom's nucleus. Just as importantly, they had proved that this energy could be controlled. Fermi's primitive furnace was the world's first nuclear reactor.

The Manhattan Project

The success of that experiment convinced the War Department that an atomic weapon could be built. Shortly afterward Fermi, Edward Teller, and several other members of the Chicago team disappeared. Only a select group of military leaders and scientists knew their whereabouts.

Over the next two years, beginning in May 1943, the U.S. government conducted what may be the largest secret operation ever undertaken. Known as the Manhattan Project, it was a secret network that stretched across the United States and Canada and as far away as Africa.

In this campus laboratory, Fermi and his colleagues determined that they could stop the chain reaction by using cadmium and boron rods. Their efforts proved not only that human beings could release the energy of an atom's nucleus but that this energy could be controlled.

The Manhattan Engineer District, as it was officially called, was located primarily in three cities: Oak Ridge, Tennessee; Richland, Washington; and Los Alamos, New Mexico. In Richland, a gigantic nuclear reactor covering six hundred square miles had been built. Here, for the first time, people were producing plutonium, an artificial radioactive element to be used as fuel for atomic bombs. And in Los Alamos, under the direction of Dr. J. Robert Oppenheimer, Enrico Fermi and scores of America's most renowned physicists worked on a project that they referred to only as "the gadget."

William Laurence, a well-known journalist sworn to secrecy by the U.S. government, was the only reporter given complete access to the entire project. He was not permitted to write or speak a word about it until after the war was over. In 1946, Laurence told his story of the Manhattan Project in a series of articles that appeared in *The New York Times*. His description of his first

Under the direction of J. Robert Oppenheimer, pictured here, Fermi and others built the world's first atomic bomb at a top-secret test site in Los Alamos, New Mexico.

visit to Los Alamos offers a fascinating insight into this secret society:

>   The first person I met that night was Fermi, who was playing some kind of indoor game on the porch of the "Blue Lounge." It was the first time I had seen him for a number of years, and I was delighted to find out where he had been hiding. I tapped him lightly on the shoulder, and as he turned around and saw me standing there he burst out laughing. It was the laughter of a child playing hide-and-seek who finds himself finally discovered.

>   Inside the main room of the lounge there was much gaiety. An orchestra composed of physicists, many of them of world renown, was playing Viennese waltzes. Gaily waltzing around the room were most of the top scientists who had disappeared shortly after Pearl Harbor. I had discovered a lost world on a mesa in New Mexico.

On the morning of July 16, 1945, on a stretch of semidesert land about fifty miles from Alamogordo, New Mexico, the world's first atomic bomb was exploded. This test-firing marked the climax of one of the greatest dramas in the history of civilization. At that moment, humans began to put atomic power to work for them.

The work of Enrico Fermi, Edward Teller, Neils Bohr, and thousands of others in the Manhattan Project ended with this successful test explosion in New Mexico. The grim result of their work is well-known in history. On August 6 and 9, 1945, the only two atomic weapons ever used were dropped on Hiroshima and Nagasaki, respectively.

Ironically, Germany, the country in which the threat of the atomic bomb originated, had surrendered to the Allied forces a year earlier. Until then, most of the reports about the German

This historic photograph, taken by a U.S. Army camera from six miles away, shows the first atomic bomb tests in the New Mexican desert, where a dome of intense brilliance rose on the horizon followed by a great, billowing cloud.

atomic bomb project had been based on rumor and guesswork. Only when the Allies occupied Germany and were able to question the leading German nuclear scientists did they learn how exaggerated those reports had been. Germany, far from being ahead of the Americans in the race to produce the atomic bomb, was hopelessly behind.

Although no nuclear weapons have been used in a war since, the events at Hiroshima and Nagasaki have changed the concept of war. Since 1945, the United States and the Soviet Union have built thousands of warheads capable of detonating nuclear weapons. These new weapons are hundreds of times more powerful than the atomic bombs dropped in 1945.

If these two countries were to fire their nuclear weapons at one another, they could destroy every major city in both countries. Many scientists believe that the radioactive fallout from these blasts would blanket the earth. This would block the sun's rays and cause a "nuclear," or year-round, winter. Crops would not grow and many animals would die. It is doubtful that the human race could survive.

As alarming as this sounds, many political scientists believe that the invention of nuclear weapons has helped to prevent the outbreak of another major war. They base their belief on a theory called mutually assured destruction, or MAD. According to this theory,

A U.S. Air Force photograph shows the explosion caused by the atomic bomb dropped on Nagasaki, Japan on August 9, 1945. The U.S. had dropped another atomic bomb on Hiroshima, Japan three days earlier. Nuclear weapons have not been used in war since that time.

HOW DOES AN ATOM BOMB WORK?

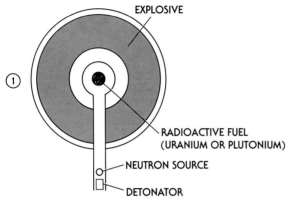

EXPLOSIVE

① RADIOACTIVE FUEL
(URANIUM OR PLUTONIUM)

NEUTRON SOURCE

DETONATOR

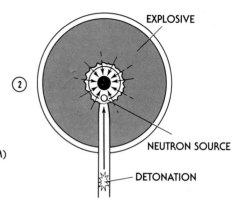

EXPLOSIVE

② NEUTRON SOURCE

DETONATION

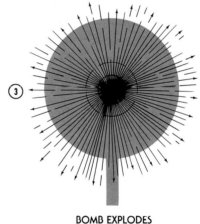

③

BOMB EXPLODES

1. An atomic bomb is a simple device that stores a mass of uranium or plutonium inside a central fuel chamber surrounded by an explosive material. The fuel chamber is large enough to permit neutrons to radiate from the radioactive fuel without triggering a chain reaction.

2. When the bomb's detonator, or fuse, is fixed, it ignites the explosive surrounding the fuel chamber. At the same time, it releases neutrons into the radioactive fuel. The explosion of the surrounding material crushes the fuel charger, so there is no longer room for neutrons to escape.

3. The neutrons fired into the fuel chamber start a chain reaction, causing the bomb to explode with a force 20,000 times greater than an equal weight of TNT.

as long as both the United States and the Soviet Union possess more than enough nuclear weapons to completely destroy the other, neither one will attack the other. In other words, nuclear weapons may make the idea of another major war so horrifying that no leader would dare consider it.

In the meantime, scientists from both of these countries continue to research and develop more powerful nuclear ex-

plosives. The desire to maintain a balance in nuclear power has resulted in billions of dollars of nuclear research. Fortunately, much of that research has also led to peaceful uses of the atom. Today, knowledge of the atom is probably the most powerful knowledge that people possess. The knowledge itself is neither good nor evil. But as you will see, it holds the key to much of our modern way of life and our future way of life.

From Swords to Plowshares

They shall beat their swords into plowshares, and their spears into pruning hooks; nation shall not lift up sword against nation, neither shall they learn war any more.

Thousands of years ago, an Old Testament prophet envisioned an age when war would become unnecessary and the tools of war would be turned into tools for production. If that age ever comes, it may be because atomic "swords" make war pointless. The destruction caused by a nuclear war would be so great that there would be no winner—there might not even be any survivors.

Although the day when all wars have ended is still nowhere in sight, we have already begun beating swords into plowshares—turning the ominous destructive power of nuclear weapons into the productive power of nuclear reactors. Because the nuclear force contains so much more energy than conventional forces, it holds great promise. The energy from the fission of a pound of plutonium is equal to the energy obtained from burning about twenty-five thousand tons of coal.

If the energy in that pound of plutonium is released in an uncontrolled chain reaction, the result is the explosion of a twenty-five megaton bomb. If it is released in a controlled chain reaction, it can provide millions of people with several days' worth of electricity. The key to nuclear energy is controlling or slowing down the chain reaction.

The way to control a chain reaction is to catch some of the released neutrons before they split more nuclei. Once you control the number of neutrons involved in a chain reaction, you can speed up the chain reaction or slow it down at will. Certain elements, like cadmium, are very efficient neutron catchers. Their nuclei soak up neutrons easily. Each of the atoms that takes on extra neutrons becomes a slightly different, but stable, isotope of cadmium. These are the simple principles on which a nuclear reactor operates.

The Nuclear Reactor

The world's first nuclear reactor was the primitive graphite block structure secretly built by Fermi and his colleagues in 1942 beneath the stadium at the University of Chicago. Although today's nuclear reactors have various kinds of safety features, cooling devices, and controls, they still operate on the same principles as Fermi's reactor. Here is the way a typical, modern nuclear reactor works:

Small fuel pellets made of a radioactive substance, usually uranium dioxide, are placed inside the reactor core. This is a large room encased in steel and surrounded by a thick layer of concrete. Once the fission process is ignited in the reactor core, the chain reaction will continue as long as radio-

U.S. Department of Energy employees work in the core of an advanced test reactor used for researching space and commercial power programs.

Worldwide Use of Nuclear Reactors

From the beginning of the Industrial Revolution in the nineteenth century to the middle of the twentieth century, coal and oil were used almost exclusively for power. By 1950, experts were warning that the world's supply of coal and oil could not last indefinitely. It was diminishing so rapidly that some experts predicted the available coal and oil reserves would be gone before the end of the twenty-first century.

Oil refineries and coal-burning furnaces also produced enormous amounts of carbon, carbon dioxide, and sulfuric waste products. Much of this waste was being released directly into the air. As alarm grew over the use of oil and coal, so did the demand for an alternative energy source. In 1950, the world's first large-scale nuclear power plant began operation in Hanford, Washington. Soon almost every industrialized nation in the world began to build reactors.

active fuel is constantly added. The heat from the fission process heats water in pipes alongside the core. This hot pressurized water is piped into a heat exchanger, where it is used to create steam. The steam in turn is directed against the blades of a turbine to produce electricity.

In this nuclear power plant in Arco, Idaho electricity first was produced in 1951.

HOW A NUCLEAR REACTOR WORKS

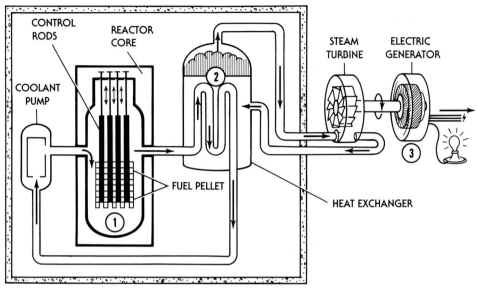

A nuclear reactor works just like a steam generator, except the heat used to make steam comes from nuclear fission instead of a coal furnace. The fission chain reaction occurs inside the reactor core, a large room enclosed in steel and concrete walls. Cadmium control rods keep the chain reaction from burning out of control. The heat produced by the fission heats a coolant (usually pressurized water) that runs pipes around the walls of the reactor core (1). When the coolant is hotter than 212° Fahrenheit, it is pumped to a heat exchanger. It boils the water inside the heat exchanger until it turns to steam (2). The steam is directed to the blades of a turbine, and as the turbine turns, it generates electricity (3).

By the mid-1990s, about one hundred nuclear reactors will be operating in the United States, supplying about 20 percent of all our energy needs. Although the United States produces more nuclear power than any other nation, most European countries rely on nuclear power for a much larger percentage of their total energy requirements. France, for example, uses nuclear power for about 60 percent of its energy needs. The use of nuclear power has reduced the world's consumption of coal and oil and helped improve air and water quality around the world.

Is Nuclear Power Safe?

Nuclear reactors have helped supply energy needs, and at least for the short term, they produce energy more cleanly and efficiently than any other energy source currently available. As the solution to the world's long-term energy needs, the promise of nuclear power almost seems too good to be true.

An aerial view shows high-level defense waste storage tanks under construction at the Savannah River Plant in South Carolina in 1978. The tanks are double-shelled, crack-resistant steel containers resting on thick concrete slabs, surrounded by a reinforced concrete wall.

Many scientists were concerned that it *was* too good to be true. Even though nuclear reactors are cleaner and more efficient that conventional power plants, they do produce waste, and this waste is highly radioactive. The radiation of gamma rays and neutrons in these materials can cause radiation sickness and cancer. Therefore, radioactive wastes must be handled with special care. They are shipped to special nuclear waste sites, where they are encased in steel or concrete. Then these containers are buried deep beneath the ground. This keeps the harmful radioactive rays from escaping.

Some scientists wonder, however, how long these containers will last. They know the material will remain radioactive for thousands, even millions, of years. Will the containers that hold the material last that long? If the containers decompose, or if the radiation builds inside until some of the powerful gamma rays penetrate the containers, the materials inside could have a disastrous effect on the world's environment.

The growing mass of radioactive waste makes many people nervous about nuclear power. They wonder whether using the inexpensive, abundant energy source is worth the risk of living with its dangerous by-products. Other scientists are certain that the methods of containing radioactive waste will constantly improve and eliminate these concerns.

Handling Radioactive Waste

Ideas for treating nuclear waste vary from sending it into space to burying it deep in the earth's crust. As yet, not enough is known about either of these environments to insure that they would be a safe place to keep radioactive waste. Some experts propose that we combine small quantities of nuclear waste with large quantities of glass or ceramic. These sheets of glass or ceramic could be placed inside steel containers. Essentially, this would be double protection. Both the steel and the glassification would keep the waste from leaking.

High-level radioactive defense wastes are stored in rooms, like this one in Carlsbad, New Mexico, carved from beds 2,000 feet below the earth's surface.

In addition, these containers would be buried several thousand feet deep in salt caverns. Salt caverns are recommended for two reasons. First, there is no water in them, so there is no risk of leaked radiation being spread by water. Second, salt is a good conductor of heat. So the heat generated by the radioactive waste would be dispersed quickly and would not have a chance to build up.

Another idea for handling nuclear waste is to recycle it. Even in the most efficient nuclear reactors, some uranium and plutonium remain unused when the fuel rods are removed. If these could be taken to a special plant, the uranium and plutonium could be chemically separated from the rest of the waste and used again. Of course, the remaining waste would still be radioactive, but with the uranium and plutonium removed, it would be much less toxic.

The problem with recycling and reprocessing nuclear fuel is that it is expensive and complex. To be economical, a reprocessing center would have to service two or three hundred nuclear reactors. The number of nuclear reactors operating in the United States would have to increase significantly before recycling would become profitable.

Assuming that effective, practical methods of handling radioactive waste can be developed, nuclear reactors still present another danger. This is the danger of an accident at a nuclear power plant. Of course, the possibility of explosions and fires at oil refineries and conventional power plants is higher than the possibility of a nuclear accident. But the consequences of a nuclear accident have the potential to be far worse.

That is why the safeguards and precautions at nuclear power plants are more extensive and more carefully monitored than at any refinery or conventional plant. They have backup cooling systems in case something goes wrong with the operating cooling system. All nuclear power plants are equipped with automatic devices that would shut off the equipment and slam enough control rods into the reactor core to com-

The Chernobyl Nuclear Reactor in the Ukraine region of the Soviet Union experienced a catastrophic accident in 1986.

If an accident does occur at a nuclear power plant, the potential for disaster is thousands of times greater than at a conventional power plant. If high levels of radiation leak into the air, people within hundreds of miles of the power plant will be endangered immediately from intense rays of radiation. In fact, such an accident has already occurred once—at the Chernobyl Nuclear Reactor in the Soviet Union. Thirty-one people were killed immediately by the intense gamma rays, and hundreds more were poisoned by the radiation—their skin, bones, and internal organs were slowly eaten away. The Chernobyl plant has been completely walled up, entombed inside thirty-foot-thick concrete walls. But the entire region, within a hundred miles in every direction of the power plant, has been abandoned because the land is poisoned by radiation.

Supporters and opponents of nuclear power think that two different lessons can be learned from the Chernobyl accident. Opponents believe Chernobyl should teach us that nuclear power is not worth the risks. It is only a matter of time, they say, before the next nucle-

pletely stop a chain reaction in case of an emergency. They have alarm and backup alarm systems to detect any overheating of the core or radiation escaping from the reactor plant.

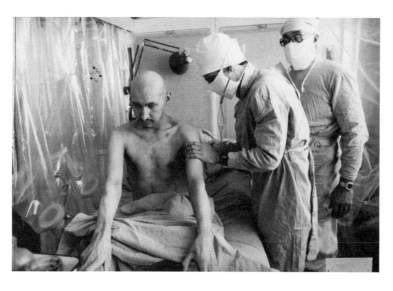

Doctors examine a victim of the Chernobyl accident. Thirty-one people were killed and hundreds of others were poisoned.

After the Chernobyl accident, Soviet workers encase the wall fracture in the fourth unit in a structure consisting of concrete blocks weighing several tons apiece.

ar accident. And that one could be much worse.

Those who support the use of nuclear power agree that the Chernobyl accident should be interpreted as a warning. Rather than a warning to discontinue using nuclear power, however, they believe it should teach us that we need to be more careful. They point out that Chernobyl was an older power plant. In design, it was much like the first nuclear reactor built in Hanford, Washington. That plant is no longer in service. Improvements in design and safety precautions that have been implemented in all nuclear plants now operating in the United States would have detected and prevented the accident.

Finally, these advocates of nuclear power point out that the world now has little choice but to continue to use nuclear power. Even if coal and oil were more desirable fuels, their supplies would soon disappear if we depended on them for all our energy needs. Some countries, such as those of western Europe, have virtually no oil reserves of

their own. Every drop of oil they burn must be imported. While the supply of uranium and other nuclear fuels lasts, these countries will undoubtedly continue to use them.

Fusion—Energy from an Abundant Source

Most nuclear physicists believe that another form of nuclear energy will make the fission reactor obsolete. They envision future nuclear reactors that produce little, if any, radioactive waste. Instead of using radioactive fuel, they will use simply hydrogen, the world's most abundant element. These reactors will not use fission to produce energy, but will use its opposite—fusion.

As we have seen, the energy in a fission reaction is released from a heavy, unstable atom when its nucleus splits. Then, some of the matter in the nucleus is converted into energy. With light elements, such as hydrogen and helium, just the opposite occurs. Energy is released when two nuclei join together, or fuse. Although fission releases enormous amounts of energy, fusion holds the possibility of releasing even more.

This is the form of energy produced by the sun. Deep in the core of the sun, hydrogen atoms are being fused together to form atoms of helium. Starting the fusion process requires a tremendous amount of heat, enough to get the protons of hydrogen moving so fast that they overcome the electrical forces that tend to make these positively charged particles repel each other. When they crash into each other, the protons fuse, forming a nucleus of helium.

Because fusion takes place at such a high temperature, scientists call it a thermonuclear reaction. So far, people have been able to duplicate this thermonuclear process only in an uncontrollable reaction. The result of that effort was the hydrogen bomb, a nuclear weapon with forces far greater than those of an atomic bomb. In fact, a small fission explosion is used in the hydrogen bomb just to produce the heat needed to start the fusion explosion.

Building a Fusion Reactor

To make fusion useful, it has to be controlled, just as fission has been controlled. That is the challenge facing today's nuclear physicists, who are trying to provide answers to tomorrow's energy needs. Surprisingly, achieving the extremely high temperatures required for hydrogen atoms to fuse is not the biggest problem. The biggest problem with building a fusion reactor is creating a container that will not melt or explode at those temperatures. Scientists are experimenting with the use of magnetic fields or "walls" of electric waves to insulate a fusion reactor.

The outcome from these experiments is still inconclusive. We do not yet know whether these forms of insulation will make a fusion reactor possible. We do know, however, that nuclear fusion or other alternative energy sources are going to be needed in the next century. Production of oil and gas cannot continue for many more years at the present rate. Even uranium supplies will eventually be used up. The promise of fusion is that its fuel, hydrogen, is abundant enough to supply the world with energy as far into the future as we can imagine.

Atoms at Work

Nuclear power is just one of the ways that our knowledge of the atom has changed the way we live. The manufacture of every artificial material has benefited by our understanding of atoms and how they behave. We have been able to harness the electromagnetic waves that are turned on and off by the atom's electrons to produce television, radio, radar, microwave ovens, and lasers. The radiation given off by radioactive materials has been put to use in hundreds of ways. Scarcely a waking moment of our lives goes by in which the discovery of the atom does not play a part.

Putting Radiation to Use

Every day, millions of patients in hospitals and medical clinics drink radioactive solutions. As these solutions travel through their bodies, doctors use radiation detectors to track them. By the behavior and movement of these radioactive materials inside the body,

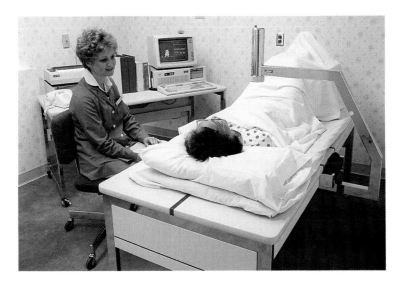

Radioactive isotopes feed this radio-isotope scanner which doctors use for early detection of osteoporosis, a bone disease.

doctors can diagnose everything from blood clots and heart ailments to gland and hormone imbalances.

Just as regularly, similar radioactive solutions are fed to plants, injected into machines, pipe walls, and other objects. In each case, people are using radioactive tracer atoms to explore the interior of a body or an object. A tracer atom is a human-made radioactive isotope, also known as a radio-isotope.

Radio-isotopes are produced by placing stable, nonradioactive substances inside the core of a nuclear reactor. There, neutrons being released by a fission chain reaction are flying madly about. Some of these neutrons are absorbed by the atoms of the nonradioactive substance. Instantly, these atoms become radioactive. In other words, they are radio-isotopes.

The element cobalt is a good example. The stable, nonradioactive cobalt atom has 27 protons and 32 neutrons, giving it an atomic weight of 59. If a chunk of cobalt is put into a reactor and bombarded by neutrons, many of its atoms will capture an extra neutron. These new atoms will still be cobalt

atoms because they still have the same number of protons and electrons. But they now have 33 neutrons, which gives them an atomic weight of 60. It also makes them highly unstable, or radioactive. These radio-isotopes of cobalt are known as cobalt 60. They are used as tracer atoms in medicine, biology, chemistry, and in the manufacturing industry.

Tracer Atoms: Finding a Needle in a Haystack

Chemists can make mixtures and chemical compounds using only a few tracer atoms mixed in with thousands of normal atoms. In this way they can make a material mildly radioactive. It is like a shepherd putting a bell on one sheep in his flock. He can trace the whole flock by the sound of the single bell.

A few tracer atoms are mixed into the steel with which motors and engines are made. Then, when engineers test these engines, they measure the level of tracer atoms in the oil or other engine lubricants. Too many tracer atoms mean that too much friction is grinding the steel.

Radio-Isotopes for Your Health

Botanists inject radio-isotopes into the water, fertilizers, and pollens taken in by plants. As they trace the movement of these materials through a plant, they learn many things about how the plant takes in water, how it uses nutrients, or how its reproductive system works. The use of radio-isotopes has led to the invention of high-production, draught- and disease-resistant hybrids of many fruits, vegetables, and grains. This is

This anthropologist works with fossils. By testing such fossils for the presence of Carbon 14, he can date them fairly precisely.

one way that radio-isotopes help improve our health.

Their use in medicine is another. Harmless radio-isotopes of sodium can be injected into a patient's bloodstream. As the radioactive material travels through the bloodstream, it is traced by a radio-isotope scanner. In this way, blood flow can be accurately timed and measured, offering valuable clues in diagnosing many serious heart problems.

Radio-isotopes of iodine are used to measure the exact size and activity of a patient's thyroid. This gland, located in the lower front of the neck, takes in iodine to produce a compound called thyroxin. Thyroxin is extremely important in helping body cells and brain cells use their nutrients properly. Radio-isotopes of iodine can reveal exactly how much thyroxin is being produced and released by the thyroid.

Finally, using radio-isotopes, doctors can use deadly gamma rays to help heal cancer patients. This treatment is called teletherapy, or sometimes cobalt treatment, because the radio-isotope used is cobalt 60. A teletherapy unit aims a narrowly focused beam of radiation from the highly radioactive cobalt 60 directly at a diseased or cancerous area either on the skin or beneath it. Because of the way the teletherapy machine focuses, the radiation can pass through the skin in a broad, harmless ray and gradually narrow to an intense beam to destroy cancerous tissues inside the body.

Nature's Clock

Radioactivity is also used to study the history of human civilization. Paleontologists have developed a method for dat-

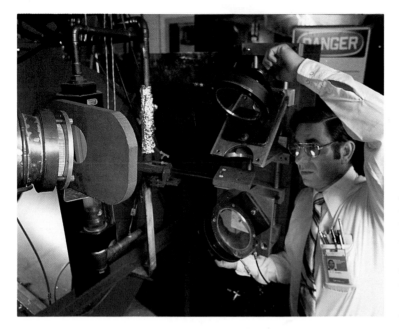

A technician adjusts the mirrors of a laser machine before conducting a metal-cutting test. Because laser light is concentrated and directional, it can cut cleanly and quickly through hard materials.

ing human artifacts and fossils based on the presence of a radioactive isotope of carbon known as Carbon 14. This isotope of carbon, which appears naturally in all living things, has a half-life of 5,700 years. In other words, every 5,700 years half of the Carbon 14 present in an object breaks down to Carbon 12, the stable carbon isotope. This fact allows scientists to determine how old something is by analyzing the proportion of Carbon 14 to Carbon 12 present.

The Wave of the Future

Our knowledge of the atom has given us an understanding of electromagnetic waves. They may take the form of visible light, radio and television waves, microwaves, and so forth. Electromagnetic waves originate in the electron orbits. As electrons leap from shell to shell, they absorb and release the quanta of energy that travel in these waves. The quanta of visible light are called photons. Radar, television, and radio depend on electromagnetic waves to carry signals over long distances. Microwaves and lasers work by using mirrors to intensify and aim electromagnetic waves.

Our knowledge of the atom gives us an energy source, a medium for communication, and a tool for scientific and industrial research. It helps us heal our bodies, and it lets us scan the past with an accurate "nuclear clock." When we look into the future, we can see the role of the tiny atom growing larger and larger.

A Glimpse of the Future

Since John Dalton put forth the first modern theory of the atom in 1803, we have taken gigantic strides in tracking it down. We now understand how the atom is structured, how it bonds to form elements and compounds, and how it can be taken apart to produce energy. Scientists have even glimpsed the elusive atom in a microscope.

The atom is far too small to be seen in a conventional microscope, but in the early 1980s, a special device called a scanning tunneling microscope was developed. It works much like a phonograph. An extremely small probe, or needle, with a tip the width of a single atom, passes over an object. Then a highly sensitive electronic device mea-

sures every up or down movement of the needle and converts that information into a picture of the object's surface. Using this microscope in 1985, scientists for the IBM Corporation were the first people to see an atom. On the microscope's monitor, the atoms appeared as little bumps.

Particle Accelerators Throw Atoms for a Spin

We should not, however, become too smug with our sighting of the atom. We have still been unable to see inside the atom, where more surprises undoubtedly await us. Though we cannot see

This scanning transmission electron microscope built at the Brookhaven National Lab in New York obtains images of biological specimens and measures the masses of proteins and nucleic acids.

OPTICAL MICROSCOPE

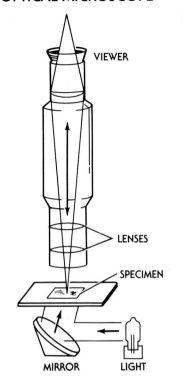

VIEWER

LENSES

SPECIMEN

MIRROR   LIGHT

SCANNING-TUNNELING MICROSCOPE

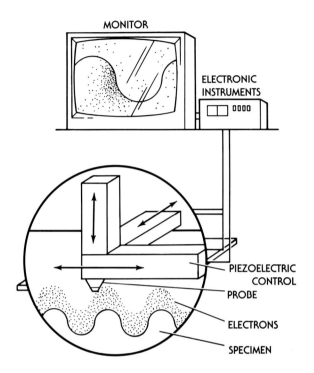

MONITOR

ELECTRONIC
INSTRUMENTS

PIEZOELECTRIC
CONTROL

PROBE

ELECTRONS

SPECIMEN

A traditional, or optical, microscope uses glass lenses to magnify visible light and produce a magnified image of an object placed beneath the system of lenses. But in order to be detected by a light wave, an object must be at least as big as a single wavelength of visible light. That is between two thousand and three thousand atoms wide.

A scanning-tunneling microscope does not rely on visible light. Instead, it uses a tiny probe that scans just above the surface of an object. With a special kind of crystal, called a piezoelectric

crystal, the probe can be moved in tiny increments, less than the diameter of a single atom.

As the probe moves between individual atoms, the electrons on the very edge of the probe move up and down in reaction to the electrons on the surface of the scanned object. These movements are measured by extremely sensitive electronic instruments, which translate the movements into a picture of the atoms on the object's surface. The picture can be viewed on a TV monitor.

inside an atom, we have made great strides in probing the insides of an atom. Rutherford's primitive neutron probes have given way to enormous particle accelerators.

Particle accelerators are designed to produce collisions between atomic particles. These collisions break up the atomic particles so that scientists can detect what they are made of. The very

Particle accelerators, like this one at the Fermi National Accelerator Laboratory in Illinois, are designed to produce collisions between atomic particles. The tunnel comprising the main ring is pictured here.

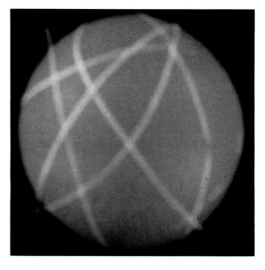

The atom is far too small to be seen with a conventional microscope. A special device called a scanning tunneling microscope, developed in the 1980's, enables scientists to look at atoms.

first atomic accelerator was invented in 1932 by two English physicists who worked under Rutherford. They were John Cockcroft and Ernest Walton. Their accelerator was about five feet long, only long enough to produce a collision between hydrogen atoms. This collision freed the electrons from the hydrogen atoms, leaving naked protons.

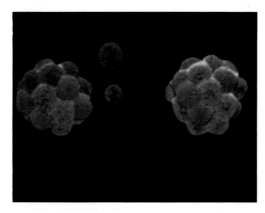

Scientists first saw an atom through the scanning tunneling microscope in 1985. It resembles clusters of little bumps.

To break up the nucleus of an atom, one must bombard it with a proton traveling near the speed of light. To accomplish this task, physics labs around the world began to build larger and larger accelerators. This permitted subatomic particles to reach the necessary speeds before they collide. The more massive the collision, the more particles are produced.

The most astonishing things began to happen when two subatomic particles, like a proton and a neutron, or two protons collided. They produced particles from within the nucleus that were smaller than the protons and neutrons. The search for the fundamental particles of nature had just taken another step forward.

Two centuries ago John Dalton had proposed that the atom was the fundamental particle. A century later J. J. Thomson showed that an atom could be divided into a nucleus and electrons. Shortly after that Rutherford identified the proton as a part of the nucleus, and then Rutherford's student, James Chadwick, found the other part of the nucleus, the neutron.

Layer after layer, scientists have peeled away the building blocks of nature. Beneath each layer they find a smaller building block. Since World War II, scientists have found evidence of dozens of particles that are smaller than neutrons, protons, or electrons. At first, this threw the science of particle physics into a state of chaos. No one could explain all these new, smaller particles, or where they came from.

Quarks Restore Order to Particle Physics

Then in 1963, two men helped restore order to the science. Murray Gell-Mann, working at Caltech Institute, and George Zweig at CERN (The European Center for Particle Physics) explained these particles. Working independently, both men reached the same conclusion: all these mysterious particles were one of three building blocks that make up neutrons and protons. Gell-Mann labeled these particles quarks, while Zweig called them aces, from the expression "Dealer's choice—aces are wild."

Zweig was right, they are wild. But it was Gell-Mann's name, quarks, that stuck. Both men had the same explanation for quarks. Protons and neutrons are both made from quarks. They identified three different kinds of quarks, which Gell-Mann labeled up, down, and strange quarks. Up quarks have a positive charge of two-thirds. In other words, the electrical charge of each up quark is about two-thirds as strong as the charge of a single proton.

A proton is made up of two up quarks and one down quark. A down quark has a negative charge of one-third. Together, the three quarks in a proton equal one positive charge. Similarly, two down quarks and one up quark combine to form a neutral neutron.

Only the up and down quarks exist in our everyday, low-energy world. The strange quark exists only in extremely high energy, such as that found in accelerators. The quark theory led to the production of the so-called big accelerators. These are enormous tracks, several miles in circumference, that carry particles at 99.9 percent of the speed of light. The largest of the accelerators in the United States is the Fermi National Laboratory near Chicago, completed in 1985. The CERN Collider in Switzerland is slightly larger.

Brookhaven National Lab staff assemble stainless steel collars around coils of a superconducting super collider used in high-energy physics research.

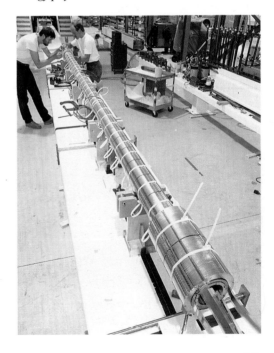

In these accelerators, more quarks have been discovered. These discoveries have led to the theory that there are actually six different kinds of quarks. Only five have been identified thus far, but the properties of these five suggest that a sixth quark, a heavy relative of the up quark, must exist. We know that the up and down quarks form neutrons and protons. What do the other quarks do? Scientists are not sure. They exist only for an instant before they are converted to energy. Most experts believe that these particles may have existed only once naturally, during the first split second after the "Big Bang"—a theory that explains how the universe was created.

One thing that scientists are hoping to learn from the collision of subatomic particles is just what did happen in the Big Bang. But even the big accelerators do not generate enough speed to duplicate the energy of that primal explosion. That is why Americans are building a super collider. They hope to pro-

duce collisions with a force that will at least begin to approach the Big Bang. This colossal accelerator is called the Superconductor Super Collider. With a track fifty-four miles long, built underground near Waxahachie, Texas, it will begin operating around 1995.

More New Particles

As nuclear physicists explore greater depths of this subatomic universe, we are reminded how many times in the past scientists believed they had found the smallest possible particle in the universe. Today we know that it is not the atom. It is not even the electron, proton, or neutron. And it is not the quark.

Particle collisions at the Fermilab, the particle accelerator laboratory in Chicago, and the CERN accelerator have demonstrated the existence of minute particles outside the nucleus. These particles are called neutrinos. Like electrons, neutrinos exist outside the nucleus

Huge magnets are used in this tunnel of the main accelerator at Fermilab. Fermilab has the largest accelerator in the U.S.

This proton accelerator in Switzerland is used to break up atomic particles.

of an atom and radiate through space. No one is sure what they do or why they exist, but scientists have found that they have no electrical charge and no measurable mass.

Neutrinos are not the only other particles physicists have detected in their accelerators. They have found a mind-boggling array of mesons, bosons, muons, and taus. Most scientists believe that these are all particles that exist outside the nucleus, like electrons and neutrinos. But scientists do not agree about what they are or do. They do not even agree on the names for these particles.

In one respect, all the subatomic particles mentioned in this book are only half of the story. For physicists now believe that for every form of matter there is a form of antimatter, a kind of mirror image that contains exactly the opposite electrical charge as its counterpart. In theory, antimatter was destroyed during the Big Bang, and, like the rare forms of quarks, it can be de-tected only momentarily after a particle collision takes place in an accelerator.

How Will New Theories Benefit the Human Race?

How many more layers of matter will future scientists peel away in the endless search for the world's smallest particles? Scientists spend enormous amounts of money each year to reveal more of the atom's mysteries. Many people question the value of these enormously expensive endeavors to solve purely theoretical problems. Will we be better off for knowing what happened at the Big Bang?

Particle physicists insist that we will. They look to the past and point out the benefits that atomic research has already brought us. They also insist, however, that their research should not have to yield practical results to be useful. The demand for practical results

The Fermi National Accelerator Laboratory in Batavia, Illinois. The largest circle is the main accelerator. Three experimental lines extend at a tangent from the accelerator. Using this huge accelerator, scientists have discovered new atomic particles.

would alter the search, and, they believe, possibly destroy it.

Nevertheless, there is already evidence that the probing of subatomic particles will have practical benefits. Methods developed for aiming neutrons in an accelerator are being applied to the field of surgery. Cancerous tissues that would otherwise be impossible to reach can be destroyed by aiming neutrons at them. The technology of superconductivity, used at Fermilab to eliminate resistance to electric current, has potential for use in fusion research, the separation of ores, and even in designing a new generation of computers that can process data at speeds approaching the speed of light.

Scientists hope that the super collider will reveal the missing quark, the so-called top quark. They are hoping it will tell them what happened at the Big Bang. But what they really hope is that it will tell them something totally unexpected. Someday people may look back on our twentieth-century theories of matter and energy with the same amusement with which we view the theories of the medieval alchemists. Says Leon Lederman, director of the Fermi National Accelerator Laboratory, "What we're really after is a new concept of reality. We're after something akin to the revolution in thinking that followed Copernicus's announcement that the earth circles the sun."

Leon M. Lederman, director emeritus of Fermi National Accelerator Laboratory, says researchers are after new information that will better explain the theories of matter and energy.

Glossary

■ ■

accelerator: A machine used to study the nuclei of atoms. It sharply increases the speeds of moving electrically charged particles, then slams the particles into the nuclei, which are chipped or split into pieces.

alchemist: A person who studied or practiced alchemy, an early form of chemistry often mixed with magic.

alpha particle: The nucleus of the helium atom, containing two protons and two neutrons.

anesthesia: A substance that deadens the nerves so that one has no feeling of pain, heat, touch, etc. in all or part of the body.

anode: The pole or piece by which positive electricity enters an electron tube.

antimatter: Subatomic particles possessing the opposite electrical charge of normal matter. Positively-charged electrons and negatively-charged protons are examples of antimatter.

atom: Any of the tiny particles of which the chemical elements are made. They are made up of smaller particles such as electrons, protons, neutrons, and quarks.

beta particle: The name used for an electron shot out from a disintegrating nucleus.

bond: An attraction between atoms that forms a stable unit, such as a molecule.

botanist: A person who studies plants and how they grow.

cathode: The pole or piece from which electrons are given off in an electron tube.

chemical reaction: A change resulting from the combining of two or more elements.

combustion: The act or process of burning.

compound: A substance that can be broken down into two or more elements.

culture: A growth of bacteria specially made, as for scientific or medical research.

decompose: To break up into separate parts.

electron: A negatively charged atomic particle.

electron tube: A sealed glass or metal container with two or more electrodes and a vacuum inside through which electrons can flow.

element: Any one of the materials that make up the world, that are not compounds, and whose atoms are all of the same type.

fission: The splitting apart of an atomic nucleus, accompanied by the release of heat and radioactivity.

fusion: The process in which the nuclei of two small atoms join to make one large nucleus, releasing energy as they do so.

half-life: The time required for half of a piece of radioactive material to decay.

immutable: Unchangeable.

inert: Lacking the power to move or act.

isotope: A form of an element that contains an unusual number of neutrons in the atomic nucleus.

matter: Anything that takes up space and has mass.

molecule: A subunit of matter composed of two or more atoms linked together.

mutable: Changeable.

neutron: A particle found in the atomic nucleus. It weighs about the same as a proton but has no electrical charge.

nucleus: The inner core of the atom, consisting of tightly packed protons and neutrons.

organism: Any living thing.

proton: A positively charged nuclear particle.

quantum theory: The accepted theory that radiation is not emitted continuously but in small, separate units called quanta.

quark: The particle believed to be the basic building block of several subatomic particles.

quintessence: The most important part of something in its purest form.

radiation: Rays and particles given off by radioactive elements such as radium or uranium.

radio-isotope: A radioactive isotope of a chemical element, used in medical therapy and scientific research.

reactor: The container in which artificial fission can take place using nuclear energy to turn water into steam, which is then used to produce electricity.

subatomic: A reference to any particle found within an atom.

teletherapy: A form of treatment using a narrow beam of radiation to destroy cancerous tissues in the body.

thermonuclear reaction: The heat energy set free in nuclear fission.

tracer atom: A radioactive atom used for the purpose of determining the position or movement of any body or substance by means of the radiation given off.

transmutation: The changing of something from one thing into another.

For Further Reading

Melvin Berger, *Atoms, Molecules, and Quarks.* New York: G. P. Putnam's Sons, 1986.

R. Hobart Ellis, Jr., *Knowing the Atomic Nucleus.* New York: Lothrop, Lee & Shepard Company, 1973.

Harold Fritzch, *Quarks, the Stuff of Matter.* New York: Basic Books, Inc., 1983.

Heinz Haber, *The Walt Disney Story of Our Friend the Atom.* New York: Golden Press, 1961.

Dan Halacy, *Nuclear Energy.* New York: Franklin Watts, 1984.

Margaret O. Hyde, *Molecules Today and Tomorrow.* New York: McGraw-Hill Book Company, 1963.

Christopher Lampton, *Fusion, the Eternal Flame.* New York: Franklin Watts, 1982.

Robin McKie, *Nuclear Power.* New York: Gloucester Press, 1985.

David Reuben Michelson, *Atomic Energy for Human Needs.* New York: Julian Messner, 1973.

Works Consulted

Isaac Asimov, *Inside the Atom.* New York: Abelard-Schuman, 1966.

John Boslough, "Worlds Within the Atom," *National Geographic,* May 1985.

Milton Dank, *Albert Einstein.* New York: Franklin Watts, 1983.

Roy A. Gallant, *Explorers of the Atom.* Garden City, New York: Doubleday & Company, Inc., 1974.

Ronald J. Gillespie, et al., *Chemistry.* Boston: Allyn and Bacon, Inc., 1986.

Vivian Grey, *The Invisible Giants.* Boston: Little, Brown and Company, 1969.

T. A. Heppenheimer, *The Man-Made Sun: The Quest for Fusion Power.* Boston: Little, Brown and Company, 1984.

Burt Hirschfeld, *A Cloud over Hiroshima.* New York: Julian Messner, 1967.

Christopher Lampton, *Fusion, the Eternal Flame.* New York: Franklin Watts, 1982.

William L. Laurence, *Men and Atoms.* New York: Simon and Schuster, 1959.

D. P. Mellor, *The Evolution of the Atomic Theory.* Amsterdam, The Netherlands: Elsevier Publishing Company, 1971.

Dinah Moché, *Radiation: Benefits/Dangers.* New York: Franklin Watts, 1979.

The New York Times, Hiroshima Plus 20. New York: Delacorte Press, 1965.

Laurence Pringle, *Radiation: Waves & Particles/ Benefits & Risks.* Hillside, NJ: Enslow Publishers, 1983.

Charles-Albert Reichen, *A History of Chemistry.* New York: Hawthorn Books, Inc., 1963.

Alfred Romer, *The Restless Atom.* New York: Dover Publications, Inc., 1960.

Index

About the Author

Timothy Levi Biel was born and raised in eastern Montana. A graduate of Rocky Mountain College, he received a Ph.D. in literary studies from Washington State University.

He is the author of numerous nonfiction books, many of which are part of the highly acclaimed Zoobooks series for young readers. In addition, he has written *The Black Death: World Disasters,* and several other books for Lucent Books.

Picture Credits

Cover photo; Michael Gilbert–Science Photo Library

AIP Niels Bohr Library, 44, 45 (both), 59

AP/Wide World Photos, 64 (top), 67 (bottom), 78

American Nuclear Society, 48

Courtesy Argonne National Laboratory, 65 (top)

The Bettmann Archive, 12, 16 (bottom), 18 (top), 19 (left), 20 (both), 22 (top left and bottom), 23, 24, 25, 26, 30 (top), 33 (both), 35, 39 (top), 50, 60 (top), 61, 63

Department of Energy, Richland, Washington, 70 (bottom), 77

Courtesy Fermi National Accelerator Laboratory, 84, 86, 87

Frost Publishing Group (Helena Frost Associates, New York, NY), 16 (top), 38, 85

Courtesy Dr. Robert Gale, 74 (bottom)

The Granger Collection, 17 (bottom)

The Image Works, 34

Lawrence Berkeley National Laboratory, 37 (both), 41, 57

Courtesy Lawrence Livermore Laboratory, 46

Library of Congress, 29

Los Alamos Scientific Laboratory, 66

The National Archives, 60 (bottom)

National Museum of American History, 30 (bottom), 31 (top), 82 (top left)

Novosti Press Agency, 74 (top), 75

Photo Researchers Inc., Ray Ellis, 79

Pictorial Collection, California Academy of Sciences, 13, 17 (top), 18 (bottom), 19 (right), 22 (top right), 31 (bottom), 39 (bottom)

Picture Book of Devils, Demons, and Witchcraft by Ernest and Johanna Lehner, Dover Publications, 15

Joseph Regenstein Library, University of Chicago, 65 (bottom)

United Press International, 67 (top)

United States Council on Energy Awareness, Washington, DC, 70 (top), 82 (top right and bottom)

United States Department of Energy, 54, 64 (bottom), 72, 73, 80, 83

Westinghouse Atomic Power/Frost Publishing Group, 56